Stochastic Sorcerers: Naive Bayes Classifiers

Jamie Flux

https://www.linkedin.com/company/golden-dawn-engineering/

Collaborate with Us!

Have an innovative business idea or a project you'd like to collaborate on?
We're always eager to explore new opportunities for growth and partnership.
Please feel free to reach out to us at:

https://www.linkedin.com/company/golden-dawn-engineering/

We look forward to hearing from you!

Contents

Chapter 1

Spam Email Filtering with Multinomial Naive Bayes

In this chapter, you will build a classic spam filter using Multinomial Naive Bayes in Python. The main steps include:

- Cleaning and tokenizing raw text data from a labeled spam/ham dataset.

- Converting the tokens into numerical features using either `CountVectorizer` or TF-IDF.

- Instantiating a `MultinomialNB` model and fitting it on the training set.

- Predicting on the test set and evaluating performance metrics.

- Adjusting the smoothing parameter (`alpha`) to achieve better generalization.

Python Code Snippet

```python
import pandas as pd
import numpy as np
import re
```

```python
import string
from sklearn.feature_extraction.text import CountVectorizer,
↪   TfidfVectorizer
from sklearn.model_selection import train_test_split, GridSearchCV
from sklearn.naive_bayes import MultinomialNB
from sklearn.metrics import classification_report, confusion_matrix,
↪   accuracy_score


def clean_text(text):
    """
    A simple text-cleaning function that:
      - Converts to lowercase
      - Removes punctuation
      - Strips whitespace
    """
    text = text.lower()  # convert to lowercase
    text = re.sub(f'[{re.escape(string.punctuation)}]', '', text)  #
    ↪   remove punctuation
    text = text.strip()  # remove leading/trailing whitespace
    return text


def main():
    # ----------------------------------------------------------
    # 1) Load and explore the dataset
    # ----------------------------------------------------------
    # Assumes the file is named "spam.csv" with columns
    ↪   ["label","text"]
    # If you have a different file structure, please adjust
    ↪   accordingly.
    df = pd.read_csv('spam.csv', encoding='latin-1')

    # For typical spam dataset from Kaggle, you might see extraneous
    ↪   columns, keep only relevant.
    # Example layout: "v1" (label) and "v2" (text)
    if 'v1' in df.columns and 'v2' in df.columns:
        df = df[['v1', 'v2']]
        df.rename(columns={'v1': 'label', 'v2': 'text'},
        ↪   inplace=True)

    # Basic checks
    print("Dataset head:")
    print(df.head(), "\n")

    # ----------------------------------------------------------
    # 2) Data preprocessing
    # ----------------------------------------------------------
    # Map the labels (spam or ham) to a binary encoding if needed
    # For convenience: spam -> 1, ham -> 0
    label_map = {'spam': 1, 'ham': 0}
    df['label'] = df['label'].map(label_map)
```

7

```python
# Clean the text
df['cleaned_text'] = df['text'].apply(clean_text)

# ----------------------------------------------------------------
# 3) Train-test split
# ----------------------------------------------------------------
X = df['cleaned_text']
y = df['label']

X_train, X_test, y_train, y_test = train_test_split(
    X,
    y,
    test_size=0.2,
    random_state=42,
    stratify=y
)

# ----------------------------------------------------------------
# 4) Feature extraction (Vectorization)
# ----------------------------------------------------------------
# Option A: CountVectorizer
# vectorizer = CountVectorizer()

# Option B: TfidfVectorizer
vectorizer = TfidfVectorizer()

# Fit on training data and transform both train and test
X_train_vec = vectorizer.fit_transform(X_train)
X_test_vec = vectorizer.transform(X_test)

# ----------------------------------------------------------------
# 5) Training a basic MultinomialNB
# ----------------------------------------------------------------
nb_clf = MultinomialNB()
nb_clf.fit(X_train_vec, y_train)

# ----------------------------------------------------------------
# 6) Initial evaluation
# ----------------------------------------------------------------
y_pred = nb_clf.predict(X_test_vec)
print("Initial Evaluation:")
print("Accuracy:", accuracy_score(y_test, y_pred))
print("Confusion Matrix:\n", confusion_matrix(y_test, y_pred))
print("Classification Report:\n", classification_report(y_test,
↪   y_pred))

# ----------------------------------------------------------------
# 7) Adjusting alpha (smoothing parameter) via grid search
# ----------------------------------------------------------------
param_grid = {'alpha': [0.1, 0.5, 1.0, 2.0, 5.0]}
grid_search = GridSearchCV(MultinomialNB(), param_grid, cv=5,
↪   scoring='accuracy')
grid_search.fit(X_train_vec, y_train)
```

```
best_alpha = grid_search.best_params_['alpha']
print("\nBest alpha from grid search:", best_alpha)

# ------------------------------------------------------------
# 8) Retrain with the best alpha
# ------------------------------------------------------------
nb_best = MultinomialNB(alpha=best_alpha)
nb_best.fit(X_train_vec, y_train)

y_pred_best = nb_best.predict(X_test_vec)
print("\nEvaluation with best alpha:")
print("Accuracy:", accuracy_score(y_test, y_pred_best))
print("Confusion Matrix:\n", confusion_matrix(y_test,
↪  y_pred_best))
print("Classification Report:\n", classification_report(y_test,
↪  y_pred_best))


if __name__ == "__main__":
    main()
```

Key Implementation Details:

- **Data Cleaning and Preprocessing:** The `clean_text` function lowercases text, removes punctuation, and trims whitespace.

- **Vectorization:** In this example, `TfidfVectorizer` is used to convert text to numerical features. Alternatively, `CountVectorizer` can also be applied.

- **MultinomialNB Model:** We call `fit` on training data and then `predict` on the test set. The parameter `alpha` controls smoothing.

- **Model Evaluation:** We calculate accuracy, confusion matrix, and a `classification_report` to measure precision, recall, and F1-score.

- **Hyperparameter Tuning:** Grid search over `alpha` shows how different smoothing levels affect generalization performance.

- **Pipeline Overview:** The `main` function orchestrates data loading, preprocessing, feature extraction, model training, and final evaluation. This structure makes it straightforward to adapt the code for other text classification tasks.

Chapter 2

Product Review Sentiment Analysis with Bernoulli Naive Bayes

Here, we will focus on classifying product reviews into positive or negative categories. We:

- Gather a dataset of labeled reviews.

- Preprocess the text by lowercasing, removing punctuation, and optionally discarding common stop words.

- Employ a Bernoulli Naive Bayes classifier, which is well-suited for binary feature representations (e.g., word presence).

- Vectorize the data, train the model, and interpret the sentiment results.

- Discuss common approaches to handle overfitting, such as tuning smoothing parameters.

Python Code Snippet

```
import pandas as pd
import re
```

```python
import string
from sklearn.model_selection import train_test_split
from sklearn.feature_extraction.text import CountVectorizer
from sklearn.naive_bayes import BernoulliNB
from sklearn.metrics import classification_report, confusion_matrix


# -------------------------------------------------------------
# 1) Sample Dataset Creation
# -------------------------------------------------------------
data = {
    "review": [
        "I love this product, it's fantastic!",
        "Completely terrible, would not buy again!",
        "Just okay, nothing special.",
        "Excellent value, highly recommend it to everyone!",
        "Worst purchase ever, it broke after one day.",
        "Amazing quality and it arrived quickly.",
        "Horrible experience. The product was faulty from day one.",
        "Satisfactory item. Not the best, but does the job.",
        "Highly disappointing, I want a refund.",
        "Great! I'm extremely happy with this purchase."
    ],
    # 1 for Positive, 0 for Negative
    "sentiment": [1, 0, 1, 1, 0, 1, 0, 1, 0, 1]
}

df = pd.DataFrame(data)


# -------------------------------------------------------------
# 2) Text Preprocessing Function
# -------------------------------------------------------------
def preprocess_text(text):
    """
    Convert text to lowercase, remove punctuation,
    and potentially remove stop words if desired.
    """
    text = text.lower()
    # Remove punctuation using a simple regex
    text = re.sub(f"[{re.escape(string.punctuation)}]", "", text)
    return text

# Apply preprocessing to the 'review' column
df["cleaned_review"] = df["review"].apply(preprocess_text)


# -------------------------------------------------------------
# 3) Train/Test Split
# -------------------------------------------------------------
# Extract features and labels
X = df["cleaned_review"].values
y = df["sentiment"].values

# Split the dataset into training and test sets
X_train, X_test, y_train, y_test = train_test_split(
```

12

```python
    X, y, test_size=0.2, random_state=42
)

# ------------------------------------------------------------
# 4) Vectorization with CountVectorizer (Binary Presence)
# ------------------------------------------------------------
# We set binary=True to capture presence (1) or absence (0) of words
vectorizer = CountVectorizer(binary=True, stop_words='english')
X_train_vec = vectorizer.fit_transform(X_train)
X_test_vec = vectorizer.transform(X_test)

# ------------------------------------------------------------
# 5) Bernoulli Naive Bayes Classifier Training
# ------------------------------------------------------------
# alpha is the smoothing parameter
nb_classifier = BernoulliNB(alpha=1.0)
nb_classifier.fit(X_train_vec, y_train)

# ------------------------------------------------------------
# 6) Evaluation on the Test Set
# ------------------------------------------------------------
y_pred = nb_classifier.predict(X_test_vec)

print("Classification Report:")
print(classification_report(y_test, y_pred))

print("Confusion Matrix:")
print(confusion_matrix(y_test, y_pred))

# ------------------------------------------------------------
# 7) Usage Example: Predict on New Samples
# ------------------------------------------------------------
new_reviews = [
    "Absolutely loved it! Will definitely recommend.",
    "Terrible experience, waste of money."
]

# Preprocess these new reviews
new_reviews_cleaned = [preprocess_text(review) for review in
↪  new_reviews]
new_reviews_vec = vectorizer.transform(new_reviews_cleaned)

predictions = nb_classifier.predict(new_reviews_vec)
for review, label in zip(new_reviews, predictions):
    sentiment_str = "Positive" if label == 1 else "Negative"
    print(f"Review: '{review}' => Predicted Sentiment:
↪  {sentiment_str}")
```

Key Implementation Details:

- **Data Preprocessing:** We rely on `preprocess_text` to lowercase and remove punctuation. This helps standardize the text data.

- **Feature Representation:** By using `CountVectorizer` with `binary=True`, we transform each document into a binary presence/absence vector suitable for Bernoulli Naive Bayes.

- **Bernoulli Naive Bayes:** We instantiate `BernoulliNB` for a binary feature space. Adjusting its `alpha` parameter (smoothing) can help mitigate overfitting.

- **Model Training:** We call `fit` on the training vectors to learn the conditional probabilities of words given each sentiment class.

- **Evaluation:** We generate predictions using `predict`, then measure performance with `classification_report` and `confusion_matrix`, assessing precision, recall, F1-score, and accuracy.

- **Handling Overfitting:** Tuning `alpha` or removing infrequent words (e.g., adjusting min_df or max_df in `CountVectorizer`) can help control overfitting. Pruning stop words can also reduce noise.

Chapter 3

News Article Topic Classification

In this chapter, you will build a topic classifier for news articles using Multinomial Naive Bayes. You will explore obtaining a labeled dataset of articles spanning different categories (e.g., sports, technology, politics). After cleaning and tokenizing text, you will transform the tokens into word-frequency features or TF-IDF vectors. Using scikit-learn's MultinomialNB, you will train and validate a model that can label new articles with the correct topic. Python code will walk through the entire classification pipeline, discussing how to handle potentially large datasets efficiently.

- First, gather or load a labeled dataset of news articles, ensuring each article has a specified topic category (e.g., "sports," "technology," "politics," etc.).

- Next, pre-process these raw texts by removing unnecessary punctuation, normalizing case, and possibly removing stop words or infrequent tokens.

- Convert the cleaned text into numeric representations, either using word count frequencies (CountVectorizer) or TF-IDF scores.

- Split the data into training and test sets and instantiate `MultinomialNB` from `scikit-learn`.

- Optionally, tune hyperparameters such as `alpha` for smoothing or apply cross-validation for robust model selection.

- Finally, evaluate the trained classifier on held-out data or new incoming articles and measure the accuracy or other metrics such as precision and recall.

Python Code Snippet

```python
import re
import string
from sklearn.datasets import fetch_20newsgroups
from sklearn.model_selection import train_test_split, GridSearchCV
from sklearn.feature_extraction.text import TfidfVectorizer,
↪   CountVectorizer
from sklearn.naive_bayes import MultinomialNB
from sklearn.pipeline import Pipeline
from sklearn.metrics import classification_report, accuracy_score,
↪   confusion_matrix
import numpy as np

def custom_text_cleaning(text):
    """
    Custom function to clean text by removing extra punctuation,
    URLs, and controlling for capitalization. Can be extended to
    remove stop words or perform lemmatization if desired.
    """
    # Remove URLs
    text = re.sub(r"http\S+|www\S+|https\S+", "", text)

    # Remove leading/trailing whitespace and set to lowercase
    text = text.strip().lower()

    # Remove punctuation
    text = text.translate(str.maketrans("", "", string.punctuation))

    return text

def main():
    """
    Main function that:
    1) Loads a subset of 20 Newsgroups data (as example),
    2) Cleans text,
    3) Builds a pipeline with Tfidf/Count vectorization +
    ↪   MultinomialNB,
    4) Optionally tunes alpha hyperparameter,
    5) Evaluates on a test set,
    6) Prints results (accuracy, classification report, confusion
    ↪   matrix).
    """
    # 1. Load dataset (20 newsgroups), focusing on a subset of
    ↪   categories for demonstration
```

```python
categories = ['rec.sport.baseball', 'sci.electronics',
  'comp.sys.mac.hardware', 'talk.politics.misc']
data = fetch_20newsgroups(subset='all', categories=categories,
  remove=('headers', 'footers', 'quotes'))
texts, labels = data.data, data.target

# 2. Clean all text samples
cleaned_texts = [custom_text_cleaning(doc) for doc in texts]

# 3. Train-test split
X_train, X_test, y_train, y_test = train_test_split(
    cleaned_texts,
    labels,
    test_size=0.2,
    random_state=42,
    stratify=labels
)

# 4. Pipeline with TF-IDF or Count Vectorization + MultinomialNB
# Here we choose TF-IDF by default. Switching to CountVectorizer
#   is trivial.
# Emphasize the Naive Bayes step for demonstration.
pipeline = Pipeline([
    ('tfidf', TfidfVectorizer()),
    ('nb', MultinomialNB())
])

# 5. Example hyperparameter tuning with GridSearchCV
param_grid = {
    'tfidf__ngram_range': [(1,1), (1,2)],
    'tfidf__min_df': [1, 2],
    'nb__alpha': [0.1, 1.0, 2.0]
}

grid_search = GridSearchCV(
    estimator=pipeline,
    param_grid=param_grid,
    scoring='accuracy',
    cv=3,
    n_jobs=-1,
    verbose=1
)

# Fit the grid to training data
grid_search.fit(X_train, y_train)

print("Best Parameters from Grid Search:")
print(grid_search.best_params_)
print("\nBest CV Accuracy:
  {:.3f}\n".format(grid_search.best_score_))

best_model = grid_search.best_estimator_
```

```
# 6. Evaluate on the test set
y_pred = best_model.predict(X_test)

print("Test Accuracy: {:.3f}".format(accuracy_score(y_test,
↪  y_pred)))
print("\nClassification Report:")
print(classification_report(y_test, y_pred,
↪  target_names=data.target_names))

# Compute and display a confusion matrix
conf_mat = confusion_matrix(y_test, y_pred)
print("Confusion Matrix (rows=actual, cols=predicted):")
print(conf_mat)

if __name__ == "__main__":
    main()
```

Key Implementation Details:

- **Text Cleaning and Tokenization:** We define `custom_text_cleaning` to remove URLs, punctuation, and excessive whitespace. This step can be customized to meet dataset needs (e.g., removing stop words, performing lemmatization).

- **Vectorization:** We use `TfidfVectorizer` by default, but switching to `CountVectorizer` is trivial, illustrating how to handle both raw frequency and TF-IDF encoding for words.

- **MultinomialNB:** The pipeline includes a `MultinomialNB` classifier. Hyperparameters such as `alpha` (Laplace smoothing) significantly impact results in text tasks.

- **Hyperparameter Search:** We demonstrate an optional `GridSearchCV` approach, allowing users to try different `ngram_range`, `min_df`, and `alpha` values to find the optimal configuration.

- **Evaluation:** We measure accuracy via `accuracy_score` and provide a `classification_report` (precision, recall, and f1-scores). The `confusion_matrix` helps visualize misclassifications.

- **Large Datasets:** For large-scale corpora, the pipeline remains the same, but consider streaming data approaches or distributed frameworks if memory constraints arise.

Chapter 4

Fake News Detection Using Naive Bayes

This approach includes the following steps:

- Preprocess headlines and body text to create robust text features.

- Vectorize the textual data using `CountVectorizer`, capturing word occurrences.

- Train a Naive Bayes model to separate misinformation from factual content.

- Evaluate the model's accuracy and analyze misclassifications to refine the solution.

Python Code Snippet

```python
import pandas as pd
import numpy as np
import re
import string
from sklearn.feature_extraction.text import CountVectorizer
from sklearn.model_selection import train_test_split
from sklearn.naive_bayes import MultinomialNB
from sklearn.metrics import accuracy_score, classification_report,
↪   confusion_matrix

def clean_text(text):
```

```python
    """
    Remove punctuation, URLs, and other unwelcome tokens from the
    ↪    text.
    """
    # Remove URLs
    text = re.sub(r'http\S+|www\S+|https\S+', '', text,
    ↪    flags=re.MULTILINE)

    # Remove punctuation
    text = text.translate(str.maketrans('', '', string.punctuation))

    # Convert to lowercase
    text = text.lower()
    return text

def load_data(filepath):
    """
    Load the CSV data containing news articles with columns:
    title, text, and label (e.g., 'fake' or 'real').
    Returns a pandas DataFrame with necessary columns.
    """
    df = pd.read_csv(filepath)

    # Drop any rows without required information
    df.dropna(subset=['title', 'text', 'label'], inplace=True)
    return df

def analyze_misclassifications(X_test, y_test, y_pred, corpus,
↪    num_samples=5):
    """
    Display some examples of misclassified articles for
    ↪    post-analysis.
    """
    misclassified_indices = np.where(y_test != y_pred)[0]
    if len(misclassified_indices) == 0:
        print("No misclassifications to display!")
        return

    print(f"Displaying {min(num_samples,
    ↪    len(misclassified_indices))} misclassified samples:")
    for idx in misclassified_indices[:num_samples]:

        ↪    print("-------------------------------------------------------")
        print(f"Predicted: {y_pred[idx]} | Actual: {y_test[idx]}")
        print(f"Article excerpt:\n{corpus[idx][:300]}...")

        ↪    print("-------------------------------------------------------")

def main():
    # -----------------------------------------------------------
    # 1) Load and preprocess data
    # -----------------------------------------------------------
```

```python
filepath = "fake_or_real_news.csv"  # Example CSV with columns:
↪   title, text, label
df = load_data(filepath)

# Combine title and text for a more comprehensive feature
↪   representation
df['combined_text'] = df['title'].astype(str) + " " +
↪   df['text'].astype(str)

# Clean up the combined text
df['cleaned'] = df['combined_text'].apply(clean_text)

# ----------------------------------------------------------------
# 2) Vectorize text data
# ----------------------------------------------------------------
vectorizer = CountVectorizer(stop_words='english',
↪   max_features=10000)
X_features = vectorizer.fit_transform(df['cleaned'].values)

# Label encoding: assume two classes like "fake" or "real"
y_labels = df['label'].values

# ----------------------------------------------------------------
# 3) Split into training and test sets
# ----------------------------------------------------------------
X_train, X_test, y_train, y_test = train_test_split(
    X_features,
    y_labels,
    test_size=0.2,
    random_state=42,
    stratify=y_labels
)

# ----------------------------------------------------------------
# 4) Train a Naive Bayes model
# ----------------------------------------------------------------
model = MultinomialNB(alpha=1.0)
model.fit(X_train, y_train)

# ----------------------------------------------------------------
# 5) Evaluate performance
# ----------------------------------------------------------------
y_pred = model.predict(X_test)
accuracy = accuracy_score(y_test, y_pred)
print(f"Accuracy: {accuracy:.4f}")
print("Classification Report:")
print(classification_report(y_test, y_pred))
print("Confusion Matrix:")
print(confusion_matrix(y_test, y_pred))

# ----------------------------------------------------------------
# 6) Analyze misclassifications
# ----------------------------------------------------------------
```

```
corpus_test = df['cleaned'].iloc[X_test.indices if
↪   hasattr(X_test, 'indices') else X_test.indices].values \
            if hasattr(X_test, 'indices') else
            ↪   df['cleaned'].iloc[X_test.nonzero()[0]].values

# Note: some vectorizers/dataset splits store indices
↪   differently
# The above line attempts to retrieve corresponding texts.
# If needed, directly reference df based on the split indices
↪   you've created.

# Because we used train_test_split on the dataset indices, let's
↪   do a simpler approach:
# We'll reconstruct indices from the original DataFrame for
↪   clarity:

# Let's re-split with the same random state to track indices,
↪   ensuring we highlight the correct text
_, test_indices = train_test_split(
    df.index,
    test_size=0.2,
    random_state=42,
    stratify=df['label']
)
test_indices = sorted(test_indices)
test_texts = df['cleaned'].iloc[test_indices].values

analyze_misclassifications(X_test, y_test, y_pred, test_texts,
↪   num_samples=5)

if __name__ == "__main__":
    main()
```

Key Implementation Details:

- **Data Preparation:** We load the dataset via `load_data`, merging `title` and `text` into a single string column and then cleaning it with `clean_text`.

- **Vectorization:** We rely on `CountVectorizer` to transform cleaned textual data into a matrix of token counts. Stop words are removed and the vocabulary size is limited to optimize training.

- **Naive Bayes Model:** We train a `MultinomialNB` classifier using the frequency features. The `alpha` parameter (smoothing) can be tuned to handle unseen words and avoid zero probabilities.

- **Evaluation Metrics:** We use `accuracy_score`, `classification_report`, and `confusion_matrix` to gauge the performance on the test set.

- **Misclassification Analysis:** The function `analyze_misclassifications` helps identify which articles were incorrectly labeled, providing insights for refining data preparation or model parameters.

Chapter 5

Document Classification with TF-IDF and Naive Bayes

This chapter dives deeper into feature engineering with TF-IDF for text classification tasks. Leveraging Naive Bayes—particularly MultinomialNB—you will classify documents such as research papers or corporate memos. By using TF-IDF, you will learn how to reduce the influence of common words while emphasizing domain-specific terms. Will show how to load and parse documents, extract crucial TF-IDF features, instantiate the model, and perform iterative tuning of hyperparameters to refine classification results.

In summary, the approach includes:

- Gathering or simulating a dataset containing textual documents with labels (e.g., "research_paper" vs. "corporate_memo").

- Splitting the data into training and test sets.

- Transforming text into TF-IDF features to downweight frequently occurring terms.

- Training a Naive Bayes model (specifically `MultinomialNB`) to classify documents.

- Employing hyperparameter tuning (e.g., adjusting **alpha** in Naive Bayes) via grid search to enhance classification performance.

- Evaluating performance using accuracy, confusion matrix, and classification reports.

Python Code Snippet

```python
import numpy as np
import pandas as pd
from sklearn.feature_extraction.text import TfidfVectorizer
from sklearn.model_selection import train_test_split, GridSearchCV
from sklearn.pipeline import Pipeline
from sklearn.naive_bayes import MultinomialNB
from sklearn.metrics import classification_report, confusion_matrix,
↪    accuracy_score

# ------------------------------------------------------------
# Simulated dataset of documents: some are "research papers,"
# others are "corporate memos." Additional text examples are
# included for demonstration.
# ------------------------------------------------------------
documents = [
    "This research focuses on quantum computing algorithms and their
    ↪    efficiency.",
    "The corporate memo outlines new policies for employee benefits
    ↪    and procedures.",
    "Quantum mechanics and quantum computing are closely related
    ↪    fields of study.",
    "Today we will discuss our quarterly numbers and employee
    ↪    engagement program.",
    "In this research paper, we explore machine learning for device
    ↪    optimization.",
    "Below is a corporate announcement about upcoming compliance
    ↪    updates.",
    "Recent studies cover neural networks for text classification
    ↪    tasks.",
    "Please review the updated guidelines for travel and remote work
    ↪    options."
]

# Labels indicating the type of document
labels = [
    "research_paper",
    "corporate_memo",
    "research_paper",
    "corporate_memo",
    "research_paper",
    "corporate_memo",
```

25

```
    "research_paper",
    "corporate_memo"
]

# --------------------------------------------------------------
# Split the dataset into training and test sets
# --------------------------------------------------------------
X_train, X_test, y_train, y_test = train_test_split(
    documents, labels, test_size=0.25, random_state=42
)

# --------------------------------------------------------------
# Create a pipeline that applies TF-IDF vectorization
# followed by Naive Bayes classification
# --------------------------------------------------------------
pipeline = Pipeline([
    ("tfidf", TfidfVectorizer()),
    ("clf", MultinomialNB())
])

# --------------------------------------------------------------
# Define a parameter grid for hyperparameter tuning
# We'll tune 'alpha' for MultinomialNB and some TF-IDF settings
# --------------------------------------------------------------
param_grid = {
    "tfidf__max_df": [0.85, 1.0],
    "clf__alpha": [0.1, 1.0, 5.0]
}

# --------------------------------------------------------------
# Use GridSearchCV to find the best combination of parameters
# --------------------------------------------------------------
grid_search = GridSearchCV(
    pipeline,
    param_grid=param_grid,
    cv=3,             # 3-fold cross-validation
    n_jobs=-1,        # use all available CPU cores
    verbose=1         # print progress messages
)

# --------------------------------------------------------------
# Fit the model on the training data
# --------------------------------------------------------------
grid_search.fit(X_train, y_train)

# --------------------------------------------------------------
# Print the best parameters and score from our grid search
# --------------------------------------------------------------
print("Best Parameters:", grid_search.best_params_)
print("Best Cross-Validation Score:", grid_search.best_score_)

# --------------------------------------------------------------
# Evaluate the best model on the test set
```

```
# ---------------------------------------------------------------
best_model = grid_search.best_estimator_
y_pred = best_model.predict(X_test)

print("\nTest Set Results:")
print("Accuracy:", accuracy_score(y_test, y_pred))
print("Confusion Matrix:\n", confusion_matrix(y_test, y_pred))
print("Classification Report:\n", classification_report(y_test,
↪   y_pred))
```

Key Implementation Details:

- **TF-IDF Feature Engineering:** We use `TfidfVectorizer` to convert raw text into numeric features, reducing the impact of very frequent words that carry less meaningful information.

- **Naive Bayes Classifier:** The `MultinomialNB` model is particularly well-suited for text classification, as it handles discrete features (e.g., word counts or TF-IDF values).

- **Hyperparameter Tuning:** We leverage `GridSearchCV` to systematically vary `alpha` for smoothing in `MultinomialNB` and other TF-IDF settings (like `max_df`). This ensures an optimal combination of parameters.

- **Pipeline Usage:** A `Pipeline` simplifies the process of chaining TF-IDF transformation with the classifier. This allows hyperparameter tuning to seamlessly adjust both parts.

- **Evaluation Metrics:** We report `accuracy_score`, `confusion_matrix`, and `classification_report` to gain a broad view of classifier performance across different document categories.

Chapter 6

Political Ideology Classification from Social Media

Here, you will construct a classifier that determines users' political leanings based on tweets or social media posts. You will begin by collecting a dataset of social media profiles labeled by ideology. Preprocessing includes cleaning emoticons, hashtags, and user mentions, then transforming text with TF-IDF or word embeddings. You will train a Multinomial or Bernoulli Naive Bayes classifier to differentiate classes like liberal, conservative, or moderate. Will show how to handle real-world social media noise and how to optimize the classifier for short text. The general approach can be summarized as follows:

- **Data Collection:** Gather tweets or posts from users labeled with their political ideology (e.g., liberal, conservative, moderate, etc.).

- **Preprocessing:** Remove or replace emoticons, hashtags, user mentions, URLs, and other social media artifacts to minimize noise. Convert text to lowercase and optionally remove stop words.

- **Feature Engineering:** Use TF-IDF or word embeddings to transform the text into numeric feature vectors suitable for classification.

- **Model Training:** Develop a Naive Bayes classifier—often `MultinomialNB` or `BernoulliNB`—to learn patterns of language usage correlated with each ideology.

- **Evaluation and Optimization:** Split the data into training and test sets. Optimize hyperparameters (e.g., the smoothing parameter `alpha`) and evaluate with appropriate metrics like accuracy or F1-score.

Python Code Snippet

```python
import pandas as pd
import numpy as np
import re
import string

from sklearn.model_selection import train_test_split, GridSearchCV
from sklearn.feature_extraction.text import TfidfVectorizer
from sklearn.naive_bayes import MultinomialNB, BernoulliNB
from sklearn.pipeline import Pipeline
from sklearn.metrics import classification_report, confusion_matrix
from nltk.corpus import stopwords
import nltk


# ----------------------------------------------------------------
# 1) Optional Setup: Download NLTK Data (e.g., stopwords)
# ----------------------------------------------------------------
# Uncomment if running for the first time
# nltk.download('stopwords')


# ----------------------------------------------------------------
# 2) Function to clean and preprocess social media text
# ----------------------------------------------------------------
def clean_text(text):
    """
    Remove user mentions, hashtags, URLs, emoticons, numbers, and
    ↪   punctuation.
    Convert text to lowercase.
    """
    # Remove user mentions (@username) and hashtags (#topic)
    text = re.sub(r"@\w+|#\w+", "", text)

    # Remove URLs
    text = re.sub(r"http\S+|www\.\S+", "", text)

    # Remove emoticons or other symbols (optional, simplifies
    ↪   approach)
    # A simple approach is to remove any non-alphanumeric /
    ↪   whitespace / punctuation
```

```python
    text = re.sub(r"[^\w\s"+re.escape(string.punctuation)+"]", "",
    ↪   text)

    # Remove punctuation
    text = text.translate(str.maketrans("", "", string.punctuation))

    # Remove numbers
    text = re.sub(r"\d+", "", text)

    # Convert to lowercase
    text = text.lower()

    # Strip extra whitespace
    text = text.strip()

    return text

# ------------------------------------------------------------
# 3) Load dataset
# ------------------------------------------------------------
def load_dataset(csv_file="political_data.csv"):
    """
    Assumes a CSV file with at least two columns:
    'text' for social media posts and 'label' for political
    ↪   ideology.

    E.g.,
    text,label
    "I support universal healthcare","liberal"
    ...
    """
    df = pd.read_csv(csv_file)
    # Drop rows where text or label is missing
    df.dropna(subset=["text", "label"], inplace=True)
    return df

# ------------------------------------------------------------
# 4) Main training and evaluation pipeline
# ------------------------------------------------------------
def main():
    # Load your data
    df = load_dataset("political_data.csv")

    # Clean the tweets or social media posts
    df["cleaned_text"] = df["text"].apply(clean_text)

    # Optionally remove English stop words using nltk
    stop_words = set(stopwords.words("english"))

    def remove_stopwords(text):
        tokens = text.split()
        filtered = [t for t in tokens if t not in stop_words]
        return " ".join(filtered)
```

```python
df["cleaned_text"] = df["cleaned_text"].apply(remove_stopwords)

# Separate features and labels
X = df["cleaned_text"].values
y = df["label"].values

# Train/test split
X_train, X_test, y_train, y_test = train_test_split(
    X, y, test_size=0.2, random_state=42, stratify=y
)

# ------------------------------------------------------------
# 4.1) Create a pipeline that includes TF-IDF and NB
# ------------------------------------------------------------
# We can choose MultinomialNB or BernoulliNB
# Let's demonstrate with MultinomialNB first
pipeline_mnb = Pipeline([
    ("tfidf", TfidfVectorizer(max_features=5000)),
    ("clf", MultinomialNB())
])

# ------------------------------------------------------------
# 4.2) Grid Search for hyperparameter tuning
# ------------------------------------------------------------
# For example, we'll tune alpha for smoothing
param_grid_mnb = {
    "clf__alpha": [0.1, 0.5, 1.0, 2.0]
}

grid_search_mnb = GridSearchCV(
    pipeline_mnb,
    param_grid=param_grid_mnb,
    cv=3,  # 3-fold cross validation
    scoring="accuracy",
    verbose=1
)

grid_search_mnb.fit(X_train, y_train)

print("Best parameters for MultinomialNB:")
print(grid_search_mnb.best_params_)
print("Best cross-validation accuracy:
↪   {:.3f}".format(grid_search_mnb.best_score_))

# Evaluate on test set
best_mnb_model = grid_search_mnb.best_estimator_
y_pred_mnb = best_mnb_model.predict(X_test)

print("\n--- MultinomialNB Evaluation ---")
print("Classification Report:")
print(classification_report(y_test, y_pred_mnb))
print("Confusion Matrix:")
```

```python
    print(confusion_matrix(y_test, y_pred_mnb))

    # ------------------------------------------------------
    # 4.3) Repeat for BernoulliNB (optional demonstration)
    # ------------------------------------------------------
    pipeline_bnb = Pipeline([
        ("tfidf", TfidfVectorizer(max_features=5000, binary=True)),
        ↪   # Bernoulli often uses binary features
        ("clf", BernoulliNB())
    ])

    param_grid_bnb = {
        "clf__alpha": [0.1, 0.5, 1.0, 2.0]
    }

    grid_search_bnb = GridSearchCV(
        pipeline_bnb,
        param_grid=param_grid_bnb,
        cv=3,
        scoring="accuracy",
        verbose=1
    )

    grid_search_bnb.fit(X_train, y_train)

    print("\nBest parameters for BernoulliNB:")
    print(grid_search_bnb.best_params_)
    print("Best cross-validation accuracy:
    ↪   {:.3f}".format(grid_search_bnb.best_score_))

    # Evaluate on test set
    best_bnb_model = grid_search_bnb.best_estimator_
    y_pred_bnb = best_bnb_model.predict(X_test)

    print("\n--- BernoulliNB Evaluation ---")
    print("Classification Report:")
    print(classification_report(y_test, y_pred_bnb))
    print("Confusion Matrix:")
    print(confusion_matrix(y_test, y_pred_bnb))

    print("\nTraining and evaluation completed successfully!")

if __name__ == "__main__":
    main()
```

Key Implementation Details:

- **Preprocessing:** The function `clean_text` eliminates mentions, hashtags, URLs, punctuation, and emoticons. This helps reduce noise common in social media content.

- **Stopword Removal:** We remove frequent words like "the" or "and" by applying `remove_stopwords`. This can improve model focus on more indicative words.

- **Feature Extraction (TF-IDF):** `TfidfVectorizer` converts each document into a numeric vector indicating term importance for that particular document relative to the corpus.

- **Model Training:** We demonstrate both `MultinomialNB` and `BernoulliNB`. Multinomial handles term-frequency features well, while Bernoulli is often used on binary features (present vs. absent).

- **Hyperparameter Tuning:** We use `GridSearchCV` to optimize the smoothing parameter `alpha`. A small `alpha` typically places more weight on rare terms; larger values smooth out extreme probabilities.

- **Evaluation:** Performance is measured using classification metrics like accuracy (via GridSearchCV), and we provide a `classification_report` plus a `confusion_matrix` to interpret model errors.

Chapter 7

Sarcasm Detection with Naive Bayes

Sarcasm detection is a unique textual classification challenge. You will explore datasets labeled for sarcasm, learning how to convert tweets or text snippets into meaningful features. While this can be approached with any NB variant, MultinomialNB often works well for capturing distinct patterns of word usage. The chapter provides scripts to demonstrate morphological analysis, tokenization, feature extraction via TF-IDF, and model training. You will see how to evaluate the model's ability to handle the subtleties of sarcastic language.

- We begin by importing essential libraries (e.g., NLTK, scikit-learn) and setting a random seed for reproducibility.

- We perform morphological analysis using NLTK's WordNetLemmatizer.

- Text data is split into training and testing sets for a supervised learning approach.

- We apply TF-IDF vectorization to convert tokenized text into numerical features.

- A Multinomial Naive Bayes model is then trained to classify sarcastic vs. non-sarcastic sentences.

- Performance metrics (accuracy, classification report, confusion matrix) are measured on the test set.

Python Code Snippet

```python
# ------------------------------------------------------------
# 1) Import statements and set seed for reproducibility
# ------------------------------------------------------------
import random
import numpy as np
import nltk
from nltk import word_tokenize
from nltk.corpus import wordnet
from nltk.stem import WordNetLemmatizer
from sklearn.feature_extraction.text import TfidfVectorizer
from sklearn.model_selection import train_test_split
from sklearn.naive_bayes import MultinomialNB
from sklearn.metrics import classification_report, confusion_matrix,
↪    accuracy_score

# (If needed, uncomment the following lines if NLTK data isn't
↪    downloaded)
# nltk.download('punkt')
# nltk.download('wordnet')
# nltk.download('omw-1.4')

def set_seed(seed=42):
    """
    Sets the seed for reproducibility in Python, NumPy, and random.
    """
    random.seed(seed)
    np.random.seed(seed)


# ------------------------------------------------------------
# 2) Morphological Analysis (Lemmatization) function
# ------------------------------------------------------------
def get_wordnet_pos(tag):
    """
    Maps NLTK POS tags to the format required by WordNetLemmatizer.
    """
    if tag.startswith('J'):
        return wordnet.ADJ
    elif tag.startswith('V'):
        return wordnet.VERB
    elif tag.startswith('N'):
        return wordnet.NOUN
    elif tag.startswith('R'):
        return wordnet.ADV
    else:
        return wordnet.NOUN

def morphological_analysis(sentence):
    """
    Perform tokenization, POS tagging, and lemmatization on a
    ↪    sentence.
```

```python
    Returns a list of lemmatized tokens.
    """
    tokens = word_tokenize(sentence.lower())
    tagged_tokens = nltk.pos_tag(tokens)
    lemmatizer = WordNetLemmatizer()

    lemmatized_tokens = []
    for word, tag in tagged_tokens:
        wnet_pos = get_wordnet_pos(tag)
        lemma = lemmatizer.lemmatize(word, wnet_pos)
        lemmatized_tokens.append(lemma)

    return lemmatized_tokens

# -------------------------------------------------------------
# 3) Prepare sample dataset for sarcasm classification
# -------------------------------------------------------------
def load_sample_data():
    """
    Returns a small sample dataset labeled for sarcasm (1) or not
    ↪    (0).
    """
    sample_data = [
        ("I love waiting in traffic for hours. It's so much fun!",
        ↪    1),
        ("This coffee is amazing. I genuinely like it.", 0),
        ("Oh great, another Monday morning meeting, can't wait!", 1),
        ("The weather is terrible, I hate how warm and sunny it is!",
        ↪    1),
        ("This place serves the best food in town!", 0),
        ("I'm so thrilled to do my taxes today!", 1),
        ("I found the discussion extremely helpful", 0),
        ("Thanks for the early morning call on a Sunday!", 1),
        ("I really appreciate your help", 0),
        ("It was such a pleasure cleaning the entire house by
        ↪    myself!", 1)
    ]
    texts = [t[0] for t in sample_data]
    labels = [t[1] for t in sample_data]
    return texts, labels

# -------------------------------------------------------------
# 4) Main training and evaluation routine
# -------------------------------------------------------------
def main():
    # Set seed for reproducibility
    set_seed()

    # Load sample data
    texts, labels = load_sample_data()

    # Morphologically analyze each text
    # (We will re-join tokens for TF-IDF vectorizer, but you could
```

```python
    # also pass a custom tokenizer to TfidfVectorizer.)
    processed_texts = []
    for sent in texts:
        tokens = morphological_analysis(sent)
        processed_texts.append(" ".join(tokens))

    # Split data into train/test
    X_train, X_test, y_train, y_test = train_test_split(
        processed_texts, labels, test_size=0.3, random_state=42
    )

    # Create TF-IDF vectorizer and transform data
    tfidf = TfidfVectorizer(ngram_range=(1, 2), min_df=1)
    X_train_tfidf = tfidf.fit_transform(X_train)
    X_test_tfidf = tfidf.transform(X_test)

    # Initialize and train Multinomial Naive Bayes
    nb_model = MultinomialNB(alpha=1.0)
    nb_model.fit(X_train_tfidf, y_train)

    # Predict on test data
    y_pred = nb_model.predict(X_test_tfidf)

    # Evaluate performance
    print("Classification Report:")
    print(classification_report(y_test, y_pred))

    print("Confusion Matrix:")
    print(confusion_matrix(y_test, y_pred))

    accuracy = accuracy_score(y_test, y_pred)
    print(f"Accuracy: {accuracy:.4f}")

    # Example usage: If you want to predict sarcasm on a new
    ↪  sentence
    new_sentence = "Oh wow, I absolutely love having deadlines at
    ↪  midnight!"
    new_sentence_tokens = morphological_analysis(new_sentence)
    new_sentence_processed = " ".join(new_sentence_tokens)
    new_tfidf = tfidf.transform([new_sentence_processed])
    new_label_pred = nb_model.predict(new_tfidf)
    print(f"New sentence prediction (1 = sarcastic, 0 = not):
    ↪  {new_label_pred[0]}")

if __name__ == "__main__":
    main()
```

Key Implementation Details:

- **Morphological Analysis**: We implement `morphological_analysis` to tokenize and lemmatize each sentence using WordNetLemmatizer. This captures the root form of words, which improves model generalization.

- **Tokenization and TF-IDF**: Tokens are re-joined into strings for TF-IDF conversion, emphasizing important words. The `TfidfVectorizer` transforms the text into numeric features suitable for Naive Bayes.

- **Multinomial Naive Bayes**: The `MultinomialNB` classifier trains on the TF-IDF features to distinguish sarcastic from non-sarcastic sentences. The hyperparameter `alpha` can be tuned for smoothing.

- **Evaluation Metrics**: We compute accuracy, precision, recall, and F1-score using `classification_report`, along with a confusion matrix. These metrics reveal how well the model handles the subtlety of sarcastic language.

- **Sample Demonstration**: A small synthetic dataset illustrates the end-to-end process. Real-world sarcasm detection typically requires larger datasets, careful data cleaning, and possibly more advanced feature engineering.

Chapter 8

Language Identification with Character N-grams

Language identification classifies text by its language of origin. You will learn to assemble datasets in multiple languages and train a Naive Bayes model to discriminate among them. The key technique here is character N-gram feature extraction, which captures language-specific patterns at the character level. Will show you how to parse text, generate N-grams, transform them into numeric features, and then build the Naive Bayes classifier. You will see how to handle extended character sets and efficient data storage for multi-lingual corpora.

In this approach, we:

- Collect or generate text samples from multiple languages and store them with appropriate labels.

- Transform text into character-level N-gram features to capture language-specific sequences (including accents or special characters).

- Feed the numeric N-gram representation into a Naive Bayes classifier (e.g., `MultinomialNB`) to distinguish among languages.

- Evaluate performance with accuracy metrics or classification reports to identify how well the model generalizes.

Python Code Snippet

```python
import os
import random
import numpy as np
from sklearn.feature_extraction.text import CountVectorizer
from sklearn.model_selection import train_test_split
from sklearn.naive_bayes import MultinomialNB
from sklearn.pipeline import Pipeline
from sklearn.metrics import classification_report, accuracy_score

def generate_sample_data():
    """
    Generates a small multi-language dataset for demonstration.
    In practice, replace or extend with real datasets containing
    texts from multiple languages and ensure Unicode (UTF-8)
    ↪   encoding.
    """
    # Example texts in different languages (simplified, short
    ↪   samples).
    # Real usage should have larger, more diverse samples.
    data_by_language = {
        "English": [
            "Hello, how are you today?",
            "This is an English sentence.",
            "A quick brown fox jumps over the lazy dog."
        ],
        "French": [
            "Bonjour, comment ça va?",
            "Ceci est une phrase en français.",
            "Un renard brun rapide saute par-dessus le chien
            ↪   paresseux."
        ],
        "Spanish": [
            "Hola, ¿cómo estás hoy?",
            "Esta es una frase en español.",
            "Un zorro marrón rápido salta sobre el perro perezoso."
        ],
        "German": [
            "Hallo, wie geht es dir heute?",
            "Dies ist ein deutscher Satz.",
            "Ein schneller brauner Fuchs springt über den faulen
            ↪   Hund."
        ]
    }

    texts = []
    labels = []

    # Flatten out the dictionary into parallel lists
    for lang, samples in data_by_language.items():
        for text in samples:
```

```python
            texts.append(text)
            labels.append(lang)

    return texts, labels

def main():
    # Set random seed for reproducibility
    random.seed(42)
    np.random.seed(42)

    # Generate or load data (replace with real dataset as needed)
    texts, labels = generate_sample_data()

    # Train-test split
    X_train, X_test, y_train, y_test = train_test_split(
        texts, labels, test_size=0.3, random_state=42,
        ↪    stratify=labels
    )

    # Build a Pipeline with character-level N-gram extraction and
    ↪    Naive Bayes
    pipeline = Pipeline([
        ("char_vectorizer", CountVectorizer(analyzer="char",
        ↪    ngram_range=(1, 3))),
        ("nb_classifier", MultinomialNB(alpha=1.0))
    ])

    # Train the classifier
    pipeline.fit(X_train, y_train)

    # Predict on the test set
    y_pred = pipeline.predict(X_test)

    # Evaluate the performance
    print("Classification Report:")
    print(classification_report(y_test, y_pred))

    accuracy = accuracy_score(y_test, y_pred)
    print(f"Accuracy on the test set: {accuracy:.2f}")

    # Below we demonstrate a small usage example on new samples
    sample_sentences = [
        "Je suis heureux de te voir aujourd'hui.",
        "I love writing in English!",
        "El zorro rápido corre en España."
    ]
    predictions = pipeline.predict(sample_sentences)
    for sentence, pred_lang in zip(sample_sentences, predictions):
        print(f"Text: '{sentence}' => Predicted Language:
        ↪    {pred_lang}")

if __name__ == "__main__":
```

Key Implementation Details:

- **Dataset Construction:** We define `generate_sample_data` to create a simplified multi-language dataset. In reality, you would replace or expand this with a larger corpus of UTF-8 encoded texts.

- **Character-level N-Grams:** The `CountVectorizer` is configured with `analyzer='char'` and `ngram_range=(1, 3)` to capture substrings of length 1 to 3. This helps the model learn distinct patterns such as accented characters, bigrams, and trigrams unique to each language.

- **Naive Bayes Classifier:** We employ `MultinomialNB`, which is well-suited for discrete features like word or character counts. Its parameter `alpha` (Laplace smoothing) can be tuned to improve performance in sparse text scenarios.

- **Train-Test Split:** We split the data into training (70%) and test (30%) sets using `train_test_split` to evaluate generalization. The `stratify` option maintains the label distribution across splits.

- **Evaluation and Metrics:** We use `classification_report` and `accuracy_score` to gauge performance. Accuracy provides an overall measure, while precision, recall, and F1-scores from the classification report detail performance per language category.

- **Sample Predictions:** After training, we demonstrate language predictions on some new sentences. Replacing the dataset with genuine multi-lingual corpora and more samples will yield better insights into real-world performance.

Chapter 9

Named Entity Classification with Naive Bayes

This chapter shows how to classify named entities (e.g., people, organizations, locations) using Naive Bayes. You will begin by annotating or obtaining a labeled corpus with examples of these entity types. The tutorial steps through how to:

- Extract contextual features (such as words preceding or following the entity).

- Incorporate part-of-speech or orthographic patterns (capitalization, abbreviations).

- Build a Naive Bayes model equipped to handle possibly sparse or categorical features.

Python examples illustrate the creation of feature dictionaries and label assignments.

Python Code Snippet

```python
import random
from typing import List, Tuple
from sklearn.feature_extraction import DictVectorizer
from sklearn.naive_bayes import MultinomialNB
```

```python
from sklearn.model_selection import train_test_split
from sklearn.metrics import classification_report, confusion_matrix

# ------------------------------------------------------------
# 1) Sample data: annotated tokens with named entity labels
#    For real applications, you would use a larger, more
#    comprehensive dataset, possibly extracted from
#    annotation software or corpora.
# ------------------------------------------------------------
# Each sentence is a list of (token, label), where label
# is one of "PER", "ORG", "LOC", or "O" (none).
sample_data = [
    [
        ("Barack", "PER"),
        ("Obama", "PER"),
        ("visited", "O"),
        ("Microsoft", "ORG"),
        ("headquarters", "O"),
        ("in", "O"),
        ("Seattle", "LOC"),
        (".", "O")
    ],
    [
        ("Apple", "ORG"),
        ("was", "O"),
        ("founded", "O"),
        ("by", "O"),
        ("Steve", "PER"),
        ("Jobs", "PER"),
        ("in", "O"),
        ("California", "LOC"),
        (".", "O")
    ],
    [
        ("Paris", "LOC"),
        ("is", "O"),
        ("the", "O"),
        ("capital", "O"),
        ("of", "O"),
        ("France", "LOC"),
        (".", "O")
    ]
]

# ------------------------------------------------------------
# 2) Feature extraction function.
#    Create a dictionary of features for each token:
#       - Current word in lowercase
#       - Flag for capitalized word
#       - Previous word in lowercase
#       - Next word in lowercase
# ------------------------------------------------------------
def extract_features(
```

44

```python
    sentences: List[List[Tuple[str, str]]]
) -> Tuple[List[dict], List[str]]:
    """
    Transform a list of token-labeled sentences into a list of
    feature dictionaries and corresponding labels.
    """
    feature_dicts = []
    labels = []

    for sent in sentences:
        for i, (word, label) in enumerate(sent):
            # Build a set of features
            feats = {}
            feats["word.lower"] = word.lower()
            feats["is_capitalized"] = word[0].isupper()
            if i > 0:
                feats["prev_word.lower"] = sent[i-1][0].lower()
            else:
                feats["prev_word.lower"] = "<START>"
            if i < len(sent) - 1:
                feats["next_word.lower"] = sent[i+1][0].lower()
            else:
                feats["next_word.lower"] = "<END>"

            # We could add more features like part-of-speech tags,
            # word shape, or suffixes/prefixes for advanced usage.

            feature_dicts.append(feats)
            labels.append(label)

    return feature_dicts, labels


# -----------------------------------------------------------
# 3) Main pipeline:
#    - Shuffle/Pretend to combine small sample data into a
#      single dataset (just for demonstration).
#    - Extract features for each token.
#    - Vectorize these feature dictionaries.
#    - Train a MultinomialNB classifier.
#    - Evaluate the classifier with a classification report
#      and confusion matrix.
# -----------------------------------------------------------
def main():
    # Flatten all sentences into one list to shuffle them
    all_sentences = sample_data
    random.shuffle(all_sentences)
    # Combine them into a single dataset
    combined_sents = []
    for s in all_sentences:
        combined_sents.extend([s])  # Each s is a separate sentence

    # We only have a small dataset, but let's combine them
    # for demonstration and pretend we have separate sets.
```

```
feature_dicts, labels = extract_features(combined_sents)

# Split into train/test
X_train_dicts, X_test_dicts, y_train, y_test = train_test_split(
    feature_dicts, labels, test_size=0.4, random_state=42
)

# DictVectorizer transforms feature dictionaries into
# numeric feature vectors for the Naive Bayes classifier.
vectorizer = DictVectorizer(sparse=True)
X_train = vectorizer.fit_transform(X_train_dicts)
X_test = vectorizer.transform(X_test_dicts)

# ----------------------------------------------------------
# Focusing on Naive Bayes:
# We use MultinomialNB, a classic choice for discrete
# features like word presence, capitalization, etc.
# ----------------------------------------------------------
model = MultinomialNB(alpha=1.0)

# Fit the Naive Bayes model on training data
model.fit(X_train, y_train)

# Predict on the test set
y_pred = model.predict(X_test)

# Evaluate
print("Classification Report:")
print(classification_report(y_test, y_pred, digits=3))

print("Confusion Matrix:")
print(confusion_matrix(y_test, y_pred))

# End of main demonstration
print("Named Entity Classification pipeline complete.")

if __name__ == "__main__":
    main()
```

Key Implementation Details:

- **Feature Engineering:** The function `extract_features` constructs a dictionary for each token, including attributes like `prev_word.lower` and `is_capitalized`.

- **Vectorization:** We use `DictVectorizer` to transform the feature dictionaries into numerical feature vectors suitable for training.

- **Naive Bayes Classifier:** A `MultinomialNB` model is instantiated via `model = MultinomialNB()`, then fit using `model.fit` on the training features and labels.

- **Evaluation:** The `classification_report` and `confusion_matrix` from scikit-learn provide an overview of how well the classifier recognizes entity labels.

- **Data Example:** Our small sample data demonstrates the methodology; in real projects, you would air on more robust datasets with thorough annotation.

Chapter 10

Medical Diagnosis Classification with Gaussian Naive Bayes

You will discover how to apply Gaussian Naive Bayes to continuous medical measurements for disease diagnosis. Using a dataset that contains numeric features like blood pressure, cholesterol levels, or glucose readings, you will train the model to predict the presence or absence of a particular condition. This chapter demonstrates cleaning real-world healthcare data, normalizing feature values, and selecting relevant attributes. A Python example uses scikit-learn's GaussianNB to illustrate how to handle continuous-valued inputs for medical decision support.

- First, gather or load your dataset containing numeric health measurements. Make sure it includes feature columns (e.g., blood pressure, glucose) and a target variable indicating disease status.

- Clean the dataset by handling missing values, removing outliers if necessary, and verifying the correctness of each feature.

- Normalize or scale the relevant attributes so that all features are on comparable numeric ranges.

- Split the data into training and test subsets.

- Create and train a Gaussian Naive Bayes model on the training data, focusing on how it learns from the distribution of continuous variables.

- Evaluate the trained model on the test data, examining classification accuracy, confusion matrix, and other performance metrics.

- Use the trained model for medical decision support, predicting disease presence or absence based on new or unseen measurements.

Python Code Snippet

```python
import numpy as np
import pandas as pd
import os
from sklearn.model_selection import train_test_split
from sklearn.preprocessing import StandardScaler
from sklearn.naive_bayes import GaussianNB
from sklearn.metrics import accuracy_score, confusion_matrix,
    classification_report

def load_data(file_path="medical_data.csv"):
    """
    Load the dataset from a CSV file. If the file does not exist,
    synthetic data is generated for demonstration purposes.
    Returns a pandas DataFrame.
    """
    if os.path.exists(file_path):
        print(f"Loading data from {file_path}...")
        df = pd.read_csv(file_path)
    else:
        print(f"File {file_path} not found. Generating synthetic
            data for demonstration.")
        # For demonstration, we create a synthetic dataset:
        np.random.seed(42)
        num_samples = 200
        # Example features: blood_pressure, cholesterol, glucose
        blood_pressure = np.random.normal(loc=120, scale=15,
            size=num_samples)
        cholesterol = np.random.normal(loc=200, scale=30,
            size=num_samples)
        glucose = np.random.normal(loc=100, scale=20,
            size=num_samples)

        # Example binary target variable (0 = no disease, 1 =
            disease)
        # For realism, let it correlate with some features
```

```python
        disease_probability = (blood_pressure*0.01 +
        ↪    cholesterol*0.005 + glucose*0.01)
        disease_probability = 1 / (1 + np.exp(- (disease_probability
        ↪    - 8)))  # logistic transform
        disease_presence = (np.random.rand(num_samples) <
        ↪    disease_probability).astype(int)

        data = {
            "blood_pressure": blood_pressure,
            "cholesterol": cholesterol,
            "glucose": glucose,
            "disease": disease_presence
        }
        df = pd.DataFrame(data)
    return df

def clean_data(df):
    """
    Cleans the DataFrame by handling missing values and outliers if
    ↪    necessary.
    Returns the cleaned DataFrame.
    """
    # Handle any missing values by filling with mean
    df = df.fillna(df.mean())

    # Simple outlier handling (optional demonstration with z-score
    ↪    filtering)
    # For more advanced datasets, domain knowledge is crucial.
    for col in ["blood_pressure", "cholesterol", "glucose"]:
        mean_val = df[col].mean()
        std_val = df[col].std()
        # Example: clip values to within 3 std dev
        df[col] = np.clip(df[col], mean_val - 3*std_val, mean_val +
        ↪    3*std_val)

    return df

def normalize_features(X):
    """
    Applies standard scaling (mean=0, var=1) to continuous features.
    Returns the scaled feature matrix and the scaler object.
    """
    scaler = StandardScaler()
    X_scaled = scaler.fit_transform(X)
    return X_scaled, scaler

def train_gaussian_nb(X_train, y_train):
    """
    Trains a Gaussian Naive Bayes model given training features and
    ↪    labels.
    Returns the trained model.
    """
    model = GaussianNB()
```

```python
        model.fit(X_train, y_train)
        return model

    def evaluate_model(model, X_test, y_test):
        """
        Evaluates the trained model on the test set and prints
        ↪ performance metrics.
        Returns the predictions.
        """
        predictions = model.predict(X_test)
        acc = accuracy_score(y_test, predictions)
        cm = confusion_matrix(y_test, predictions)
        cr = classification_report(y_test, predictions)

        print(f"Accuracy: {acc:.4f}")
        print("Confusion Matrix:")
        print(cm)
        print("Classification Report:")
        print(cr)

        return predictions

    def main():
        # 1) Load the dataset
        df = load_data()

        # 2) Clean the dataset
        df = clean_data(df)

        # Separate features and target
        X = df.drop(columns=["disease"]).values
        y = df["disease"].values

        # 3) Normalize (Scale) data
        X_scaled, scaler = normalize_features(X)

        # 4) Split into train/test set
        X_train, X_test, y_train, y_test = train_test_split(
            X_scaled, y, test_size=0.2, random_state=42
        )

        # 5) Train a GaussianNB model
        model = train_gaussian_nb(X_train, y_train)

        # 6) Evaluate on the test set
        print("Evaluation on test set:")
        _ = evaluate_model(model, X_test, y_test)

        # Example usage: Suppose you have new patient data
        new_patient_data = np.array([[130, 220, 110]])  #
        ↪ (blood_pressure, cholesterol, glucose)
        new_patient_data_scaled = scaler.transform(new_patient_data)
        prediction = model.predict(new_patient_data_scaled)
```

51

```
    print(f"Predicted disease presence (1) or absence (0) for the
    ↪  new patient: {prediction[0]}")

if __name__ == "__main__":
    main()
```

Key Implementation Details:

- The function `load_data` checks for an existing dataset. If not found, a synthetic dataset is generated. In practical scenarios, replace it with a real CSV file path.

- The function `clean_data` handles missing values (filling with mean) and provides a simple example of outlier clipping based on a 3-sigma rule. This is highly dependent on domain-specific thresholds.

- The function `normalize_features` applies the `StandardScaler` from scikit-learn to standardize continuous features, ensuring that they have zero mean and unit variance.

- The function `train_gaussian_nb` demonstrates training a `GaussianNB` model from scikit-learn on the training dataset, capitalizing on the normal distribution assumption for continuous data.

- Model evaluation through `evaluate_model` reports accuracy, a confusion matrix, and a classification report, illustrating typical metrics for a classification task.

- In `main`, the entire pipeline is orchestrated: loading/cleaning data, scaling, splitting into train/test, fitting the Gaussian Naive Bayes classifier, and generating a prediction on a hypothetical new patient measurement.

Chapter 11

Customer Churn Prediction Using Naive Bayes

In this chapter, you will develop a Naive Bayes classifier to predict customer churn in industries such as telecom, banking, or SaaS. Beginning with a dataset of user demographics and service usage records, you will engineer features that highlight patterns indicating potential churn. Then, you will train a Naive Bayes model (often Multinomial or Bernoulli, depending on how features are encoded). Python code will demonstrate the best practices for loading tabular data, encoding categorical variables, training the model, and calibrating predictions to target high-risk customers.

- First, load and inspect the dataset to understand its structure. Handle missing values if present.

- Next, split the data into training and testing subsets.

- Encode categorical features so they can be fed into a Naive Bayes model (this could involve `OneHotEncoder` or `OrdinalEncoder`).

- Fit a Naive Bayes classifier, such as `BernoulliNB` for binary-encoded data or `MultinomialNB` for frequency-based features.

- Evaluate the model with metrics like accuracy, confusion matrix, and precision/recall. Consider calibrating the model outputs to better identify high-risk (likely-to-churn) customers.

Python Code Snippet

```python
import pandas as pd
import numpy as np
from sklearn.model_selection import train_test_split
from sklearn.preprocessing import OneHotEncoder, StandardScaler
from sklearn.compose import ColumnTransformer
from sklearn.pipeline import Pipeline
from sklearn.naive_bayes import BernoulliNB, MultinomialNB
from sklearn.metrics import accuracy_score, classification_report,
    confusion_matrix
from sklearn.calibration import CalibratedClassifierCV

def load_data(csv_path):
    """
    Loads the customer churn dataset from the specified csv_path.
    Returns a pandas DataFrame.
    """
    df = pd.read_csv(csv_path)
    return df

def preprocess_data(df, target_col='Churn'):
    """
    Splits the dataframe into features (X) and target (y).
    Identifies numerical and categorical columns for transformation.
    """
    # Drop rows with missing target or crucial data if necessary
    df = df.dropna(subset=[target_col])

    # Extract target
    y = df[target_col]

    # Drop target from features
    X = df.drop(columns=[target_col])

    # Identify categorical versus numerical columns
    numerical_cols =
        X.select_dtypes(include=[np.number]).columns.tolist()
    categorical_cols = X.select_dtypes(include=['object',
        'category']).columns.tolist()

    return X, y, numerical_cols, categorical_cols

def build_pipeline(nb_type='bernoulli', alpha=1.0):
    """
    Builds a scikit-learn Pipeline with data transformations and a
        Naive Bayes estimator.
    nb_type: 'bernoulli' or 'multinomial'
    alpha: smoothing parameter for Naive Bayes
    """

    # We will create placeholders for column transformations
```

```python
    # OneHotEncoder for categorical, StandardScaler for numeric
    numeric_transformer = Pipeline([
        ('scaler', StandardScaler())
    ])

    categorical_transformer = Pipeline([
        ('onehot', OneHotEncoder(handle_unknown='ignore'))
    ])

    preprocessor = ColumnTransformer([
        ('num', numeric_transformer, []),    # to be set dynamically
        ('cat', categorical_transformer, [])
    ])

    # Select which Naive Bayes model to use
    if nb_type.lower() == 'multinomial':
        nb_estimator = MultinomialNB(alpha=alpha)
    else:
        nb_estimator = BernoulliNB(alpha=alpha)

    # Pipeline: (preprocessing) -> (Naive Bayes)
    pipeline = Pipeline([
        ('preprocessor', preprocessor),
        ('classifier', nb_estimator)
    ])

    return pipeline

def calibrate_model(pipeline, X_train, y_train, X_val, y_val):
    """
    Demonstrates calibration by fitting the pipeline on training
    ↪    data,
    then using CalibratedClassifierCV on the validation portion to
    ↪    refine probability estimates.
    """
    # First, fit the pipeline "as is" on the training set
    pipeline.fit(X_train, y_train)

    # Now wrap the existing classifier in CalibratedClassifierCV
    nb_estimator = pipeline.named_steps['classifier']

    # To use CalibratedClassifierCV, we need the pipeline's
    ↪    transformations
    # We'll transform the validation data and refit a calibrated
    ↪    classifier
    X_val_transformed =
    ↪    pipeline.named_steps['preprocessor'].transform(X_val)

    calibrator = CalibratedClassifierCV(base_estimator=nb_estimator,
    ↪    cv='prefit')
    calibrator.fit(X_val_transformed, y_val)
```

```python
    # Replace the NB classifier in the pipeline with our calibrated
    ↪    model
    pipeline.steps[-1] = ('classifier', calibrator)

    return pipeline

def main():
    # --------------------------
    # 1. Load Data
    # --------------------------
    data_path = 'customer_churn.csv'  # Adjust file path as needed
    df = load_data(data_path)

    # --------------------------
    # 2. Preprocess
    # --------------------------
    target_col = 'Churn'  # Assume "Churn" is in {0,1} or {Yes,No}
    X, y, numeric_cols, categorical_cols = preprocess_data(df,
    ↪    target_col=target_col)

    # Strategy: We'll do a single train-test split, then from the
    ↪    train set, carve out a validation set for calibration
    X_train_full, X_test, y_train_full, y_test = train_test_split(X,
    ↪    y, test_size=0.2, random_state=42, stratify=y)
    X_train, X_val, y_train, y_val = train_test_split(X_train_full,
    ↪    y_train_full, test_size=0.25,
      random_state=42, stratify=y_train_full)

    # --------------------------
    # 3. Build Pipeline
    # --------------------------
    # We'll choose BernoulliNB for demonstration; alpha is the
    ↪    smoothing parameter
    pipeline = build_pipeline(nb_type='bernoulli', alpha=1.0)

    # We must set the columns to transform in the pipeline's
    ↪    preprocessor
    pipeline.named_steps['preprocessor'].transformers[0] = ('num',
            pipeline.named_steps['preprocessor'].transformers[0][1],
            numeric_cols)
    pipeline.named_steps['preprocessor'].transformers[1] = ('cat',
            pipeline.named_steps['preprocessor'].transformers[1][1],
            categorical_cols)

    # --------------------------
    # 4. Calibration
    # --------------------------
    # Fit the pipeline to the train set; calibrate on validation to
    ↪    refine probability estimates
    pipeline = calibrate_model(pipeline, X_train, y_train, X_val,
    ↪    y_val)

    # --------------------------
```

```python
# 5. Evaluation
# --------------------------
# Evaluate on test data
y_pred = pipeline.predict(X_test)
accuracy = accuracy_score(y_test, y_pred)
cr = classification_report(y_test, y_pred, digits=4)
cm = confusion_matrix(y_test, y_pred)

print(f"Test Accuracy: {accuracy:.4f}")
print("Classification Report:")
print(cr)
print("Confusion Matrix:")
print(cm)

# Show how to get probabilities and rank high-risk customers
# Here we assume 'Churn' = 1 is "positive"/"churn" class
if hasattr(pipeline.named_steps['classifier'], 'predict_proba'):
    y_scores = pipeline.predict_proba(X_test)[:, 1]
    # For demonstration, we can identify the top 5 "most likely
    ↪   to churn"
    top_indices = np.argsort(-y_scores)[:5]
    print("\nTop 5 high-risk customers in test set:")
    for idx in top_indices:
        print(f"Customer Index: {X_test.index[idx]}, Probability
        ↪   of Churn: {y_scores[idx]:.4f}")

if __name__ == "__main__":
    main()
```

Key Implementation Details:

- **Data Loading:** We use `pandas` to load the CSV file. The function `load_data` demonstrates a simple approach for reading the dataset.

- **Feature Preprocessing:** The function `preprocess_data` separates the target from features and identifies numerical and categorical columns for subsequent transformations.

- **Naive Bayes Pipeline:** We build a `Pipeline` that includes a `ColumnTransformer` for different data types (numeric vs. categorical) followed by the chosen Naive Bayes estimator (`BernoulliNB` or `MultinomialNB`).

- **Smoothing Parameter (`alpha`):** Naive Bayes models use `alpha` for additive smoothing. Adjusting `alpha` can handle zero-frequency issues in Bernoulli or Multinomial models.

- **Calibration:** We demonstrate a simple calibration approach using `CalibratedClassifierCV`, providing better probabilistic outputs for identifying high-churn customers.

- **Model Evaluation:** We compute the `accuracy_score`, `classification_report`, and `confusion_matrix`. Additionally, we show how to retrieve `predict_proba` to rank customers by churn risk.

Chapter 12

Customer Segmentation for Marketing Campaigns

Marketing professionals often segment customers to tailor campaigns. You will learn to apply Naive Bayes to categorize customers into distinct segments using behavioral and demographic data. The chapter shows how to transform raw data—such as purchase frequency, average spending, or web activity—into features suitable for the NB classifier. You will see how to group similar customers automatically, then label them with meaningful segments that can guide marketing strategies.

- First, generate or load a dataset capturing features like purchase frequency, average spend, and web activity.

- Next, preprocess and split the data into training and testing sets.

- Then, train a Naive Bayes classifier to predict customer segments based on these features.

- Finally, evaluate the classifier's performance to ensure segments are identified accurately, and observe how these segments might be used for marketing campaigns.

Python Code Snippet

```python
import numpy as np
import pandas as pd
from sklearn.model_selection import train_test_split
from sklearn.naive_bayes import GaussianNB
from sklearn.preprocessing import StandardScaler
from sklearn.metrics import classification_report, confusion_matrix


def generate_synthetic_data(num_samples=1000):
    """
    Creates a synthetic dataset for customer segmentation.
    Three segments are generated ('Segment0', 'Segment1',
    ↪  'Segment2'),
    each with distinct distributions for purchase frequency,
    average spending, and web visit activity.
    """
    np.random.seed(42)

    # Each segment gets ~1/3 of the total samples
    segment_size = num_samples // 3

    # Segment 0 (low spend, low frequency)
    freq0 = np.random.normal(loc=1, scale=0.5, size=segment_size)
    spend0 = np.random.normal(loc=20, scale=5, size=segment_size)
    web0 = np.random.normal(loc=10, scale=3, size=segment_size)
    label0 = np.array(["Segment0"] * segment_size)

    # Segment 1 (average spend, moderate frequency)
    freq1 = np.random.normal(loc=5, scale=1.0, size=segment_size)
    spend1 = np.random.normal(loc=50, scale=10, size=segment_size)
    web1 = np.random.normal(loc=25, scale=5, size=segment_size)
    label1 = np.array(["Segment1"] * segment_size)

    # Segment 2 (high spend, high frequency)
    freq2 = np.random.normal(loc=10, scale=2, size=segment_size)
    spend2 = np.random.normal(loc=150, scale=30, size=segment_size)
    web2 = np.random.normal(loc=40, scale=10, size=segment_size)
    label2 = np.array(["Segment2"] * segment_size)

    # Concatenate all segments
    freq = np.concatenate([freq0, freq1, freq2])
    spend = np.concatenate([spend0, spend1, spend2])
    web_visits = np.concatenate([web0, web1, web2])
    labels = np.concatenate([label0, label1, label2])

    # If num_samples is not perfectly divisible by 3, add random
    ↪  extra rows
    remainder = num_samples - (3 * segment_size)
    if remainder > 0:
        extra_freq = np.random.normal(loc=7, scale=3,
        ↪  size=remainder)
```

60

```
        extra_spend = np.random.normal(loc=80, scale=25,
        ↳   size=remainder)
        extra_web = np.random.normal(loc=20, scale=7,
        ↳   size=remainder)
        extra_labels = np.array(["Segment0"] * remainder)
        freq = np.concatenate([freq, extra_freq])
        spend = np.concatenate([spend, extra_spend])
        web_visits = np.concatenate([web_visits, extra_web])
        labels = np.concatenate([labels, extra_labels])

    # Build final DataFrame
    df = pd.DataFrame({
        "purchase_frequency": freq,
        "avg_spend": spend,
        "web_activity": web_visits,
        "segment_label": labels
    })

    return df

def main():
    # 1) Generate synthetic customer data
    df = generate_synthetic_data(num_samples=1000)

    # 2) Shuffle the dataset
    df = df.sample(frac=1.0, random_state=42).reset_index(drop=True)

    # 3) Split into features and label
    X = df[["purchase_frequency", "avg_spend", "web_activity"]]
    y = df["segment_label"]

    # 4) Train-Test split
    X_train, X_test, y_train, y_test = train_test_split(
        X, y, test_size=0.2, random_state=42, stratify=y
    )

    # 5) Feature scaling
    scaler = StandardScaler()
    X_train_scaled = scaler.fit_transform(X_train)
    X_test_scaled = scaler.transform(X_test)

    # 6) Train Naive Bayes Classifier
    nb_model = GaussianNB()
    nb_model.fit(X_train_scaled, y_train)

    # 7) Evaluate the model
    y_pred = nb_model.predict(X_test_scaled)
    print("Classification Report:\n", classification_report(y_test,
    ↳   y_pred))
    print("Confusion Matrix:\n", confusion_matrix(y_test, y_pred))

    # 8) Demonstrate a single prediction (sample customer)
    new_customer = np.array([[4.5, 60, 22]])  # hypothetical values
```

```
    new_customer_scaled = scaler.transform(new_customer)
    predicted_segment = nb_model.predict(new_customer_scaled)
    print(f"New customer predicted segment: {predicted_segment[0]}")

if __name__ == "__main__":
    main()
```

Key Implementation Details:

- **generate_synthetic_data**: Creates a DataFrame with features (purchase frequency, spend, web activity) and a categorical segment label.

- **train_test_split**: Splits features and labels into training and testing subsets, ensuring unbiased performance estimates.

- **StandardScaler**: Standardizes numeric features, improving Naive Bayes performance when features vary greatly in scale.

- **GaussianNB**: A Naive Bayes classifier suited for continuous data; it models each class with a Gaussian distribution per feature.

- **classification_report** and **confusion_matrix**: Provide metrics like precision, recall, and f1-score to evaluate how well each segment is identified.

- **Practical Use**: In real-world campaigns, identifying segment membership helps tailor marketing messages, promotions, and outreach for maximum engagement.

Chapter 13

Stock Price Movement Classification (Up or Down)

Switching to a financial application, this chapter reveals how to classify daily stock price movements as up or down using Naive Bayes. You will obtain historical stock quotes and relevant indicators (e.g., moving averages, trading volume). After data cleansing and feature engineering, you will train a Bernoulli or Gaussian NB model, depending on whether features are treated as binary or continuous. Implementing this workflow in Python will show the importance of sliding window approaches, alignment of features with target variables, and incremental evaluation over time.

Below is a concise step-by-step approach:

- Obtain or simulate historical price data (e.g., open, high, low, close, volume).

- Engineer features such as moving averages and daily returns.

- Align each feature vector with the next day's price direction (up or down) as the target label.

- Split data into training and test sets.

- Decide whether to use Bernoulli (`BernoulliNB`) or Gaussian (`GaussianNB`) Naive Bayes based on feature type.

- Train the model, generate predictions, and evaluate classification metrics.

- (Optional) Incorporate a sliding window or incremental learning (`partial_fit`) to update the model over time.

Python Code Snippet

```python
import numpy as np
import pandas as pd
from sklearn.naive_bayes import BernoulliNB, GaussianNB
from sklearn.model_selection import train_test_split
from sklearn.metrics import accuracy_score, classification_report
import matplotlib.pyplot as plt

def simulate_stock_data(num_days=300, seed=42):
    """
    Simulate a random walk style stock price for demonstration
    ↪ purposes.
    This function returns a DataFrame with columns:
      'Close' and 'Volume' for each simulated trading day.
    """
    np.random.seed(seed)
    # Initialize price and volume
    prices = [100.0]
    for _ in range(num_days - 1):
        # Random daily returns
        daily_return = np.random.normal(loc=0.0, scale=1.0)
        prices.append(prices[-1] + daily_return)
    # Create a random volume series
    volume = np.abs(np.random.normal(loc=50000, scale=10000,
    ↪ size=num_days))

    df = pd.DataFrame({
        'Close': prices,
        'Volume': volume
    })
    return df

def feature_engineering(df, ma_window=5):
    """
    Perform feature engineering:
      - Compute the moving average over a given window.
      - Compute daily returns.
      - Convert data into a set of features for each row.
    """
    df['MA'] = df['Close'].rolling(ma_window).mean()
    df['Daily_Return'] = df['Close'].pct_change()
```

```python
    # Because the first few rows won't have a valid MA or daily
    ↪   return, we drop NaNs
    df.dropna(inplace=True)

    # Construct a feature matrix X
    # Example features: [Close, Volume, MA, Daily_Return]
    X = df[['Close', 'Volume', 'MA', 'Daily_Return']].values
    return df, X

def build_labels(df):
    """
    Build binary labels indicating whether the next day's price
    is up (1) or down (0) compared to the current day's close.
    We shift the 'Close' by -1 to align each row with the next day.
    """
    df['Next_Close'] = df['Close'].shift(-1)
    # Drop the last row where Next_Close is NaN
    df.dropna(inplace=True)

    # Label: 1 if next day's close is higher, else 0
    y = (df['Next_Close'] > df['Close']).astype(int).values
    return df, y

def select_naive_bayes_model(model_type='Gaussian'):
    """
    Instantiate a Naive Bayes model.
    model_type can be 'Gaussian' or 'Bernoulli'.
    """
    if model_type == 'Gaussian':
        model = GaussianNB()
    elif model_type == 'Bernoulli':
        model = BernoulliNB()
    else:
        raise ValueError("model_type must be 'Gaussian' or
        ↪   'Bernoulli'.")
    return model

def plot_predictions(df, y_true, y_pred):
    """
    Simple utility to visualize a segment of true vs. predicted
    moves (up or down). This just plots the last 50 days as an
    ↪   example.
    """
    days_to_plot = 50
    plt.figure(figsize=(12, 4))
    plt.plot(df['Close'].tail(days_to_plot).values, label='Close
    ↪   Price', color='blue')

    indices = np.arange(len(df))[-days_to_plot:]
    up_predictions = [np.nan]*len(df)
    down_predictions = [np.nan]*len(df)

    for i in range(-days_to_plot, 0):
```

```python
        if y_pred[i] == 1:
            up_predictions[indices[i]] =
            ↪   df['Close'].iloc[indices[i]]
        else:
            down_predictions[indices[i]] =
            ↪   df['Close'].iloc[indices[i]]

    plt.scatter(indices, up_predictions[-days_to_plot:], marker='^',
    ↪   color='green', label='Predicted Up')
    plt.scatter(indices, down_predictions[-days_to_plot:],
    ↪   marker='v', color='red', label='Predicted Down')

    plt.title("True vs. Predicted Stock Moves (last 50 days)")
    plt.legend()
    plt.show()

def main():
    # 1) Simulate or load stock data
    df = simulate_stock_data(num_days=300)

    # 2) Feature Engineering
    df, X = feature_engineering(df, ma_window=5)

    # 3) Build Labels (1 for up, 0 for down)
    df, y = build_labels(df)

    # Align X and y shapes
    # After dropping NaN for rolling calculations and shifting, X
    ↪   and y should match length
    if len(X) > len(y):
        X = X[:len(y)]
    elif len(y) > len(X):
        y = y[:len(X)]

    # 4) Split data into train and test sets
    # For a realistic scenario, we might do a chronological split.
    ↪   Here we use random for demonstration.
    X_train, X_test, y_train, y_test = train_test_split(X, y,
    ↪   test_size=0.2, shuffle=True, random_state=42)

    # 5) Instantiate Naive Bayes model (Gaussian or Bernoulli)
    nb_model = select_naive_bayes_model(model_type='Gaussian')

    # 6) Train the model
    nb_model.fit(X_train, y_train)

    # 7) Predict on the test set
    y_pred = nb_model.predict(X_test)

    # 8) Evaluate results
    acc = accuracy_score(y_test, y_pred)
    print(f"Test Accuracy: {acc:.4f}")
    print("\nClassification Report:")
```

```
      print(classification_report(y_test, y_pred))

      # 9) Plot predictions for an illustrative window at the end of
      ↪    the entire dataset
      #     We'll combine the entire dataset X,y for demonstration of
      ↪    the final predictions.
      #     This is just for visualization convenience.
      y_full_pred = nb_model.predict(X)
      plot_predictions(df, y, y_full_pred)

if __name__ == "__main__":
    main()
```

Key Implementation Details:

- **Data Simulation or Acquisition:** This example uses a function `simulate_stock_data` to generate a random-walk-like time series. In a real application, you might load data from a file or an API (e.g., `yfinance`).

- **Feature Engineering:** The `feature_engineering` function computes a moving average and a daily return to capture short-term trends and momentum. Additional features (e.g., RSI, MACD) can be easily added.

- **Label Construction:** The next-day's closing price is used to define an up (1) or down (0) label in `build_labels`.

- **Naive Bayes Model:** The core of the solution is the Naive Bayes classifier (`GaussianNB` or `BernoulliNB`). Gaussian NB fits naturally with continuous features, whereas Bernoulli NB is ideal for binary/binned features.

- **Sliding Window Consideration:** Although this snippet performs a simple random split, real-world finance applications often use a time-based (sliding or rolling) window for training. Incremental learning with `partial_fit` may further refine the model as new data arrives.

- **Evaluation and Visualization:** We show a `plot_predictions` function to compare predicted up/down signals against the actual close prices for a sample range (last 50 days). Additional metrics like precision, recall, or confusion matrices can refine performance insights.

- **Extensibility:** This pipeline can be extended with more advanced feature engineering, external data sources, and custom evaluation strategies. Naive Bayes can serve as a fast baseline to compare against more complex models.

Chapter 14

Real-time Tweet Classification for Event Tracking

This chapter teaches you to handle streaming data in Python while applying Naive Bayes for real-time classification. You will set up a pipeline that ingests tweets about current events (for instance, disaster alerts or product launches), preprocesses them, and updates the NB model on-the-fly. You will explore approaches for online learning, where your classifier refines itself as new labeled data becomes available. Specific Python libraries like tweepy (for streaming tweets) and partial_fit from scikit-learn will demonstrate how to continuously update the model with minimal downtime.

- First, you will establish a streaming connection to Twitter using Tweepy.

- Next, each incoming tweet is preprocessed, converting text into a numeric vector representation.

- A Naive Bayes classifier is trained incrementally via partial_fit to classify tweets as relevant or not relevant to a chosen event category.

- The classifier continuously refines its parameters based on newly labeled data, ensuring minimal downtime for real-time classification needs.

Python Code Snippet

```python
import os
import re
import time
import tweepy
import numpy as np

from sklearn.feature_extraction.text import CountVectorizer
from sklearn.naive_bayes import MultinomialNB

#########################################################################
# 1) Twitter API Authentication (User must fill in valid
# ↪  credentials)
#########################################################################
API_KEY = "YOUR_API_KEY"
API_SECRET = "YOUR_API_SECRET"
ACCESS_TOKEN = "YOUR_ACCESS_TOKEN"
ACCESS_TOKEN_SECRET = "YOUR_ACCESS_TOKEN_SECRET"


#########################################################################
# 2) Simple text cleaning function
#########################################################################
def clean_tweet_text(text):
    """
    Removes URLs, mentions, and some punctuation from the tweet
    ↪  text.
    """
    text = re.sub(r"http\S+", "", text)        # remove URLs
    text = re.sub(r"@\S+", "", text)           # remove mentions
    text = re.sub(r"[^a-zA-Z0-9\s#]", "", text) # remove punctuation
    # ↪  except hashtags
    text = text.lower().strip()
    return text


#########################################################################
# 3) Real-time Tweet Stream Listener for online learning
#########################################################################
class RealTimeTweetListener(tweepy.StreamListener):
    """
    Custom StreamListener class to gather tweets in real-time
    and perform partial_fit on a Naive Bayes model as labeled data
    ↪  arrives.
    """
    def __init__(self, nb_classifier, vectorizer,
    ↪  event_hashtag="#disaster", batch_size=1):
        super(RealTimeTweetListener, self).__init__()
        self.nb_classifier = nb_classifier
        self.vectorizer = vectorizer

        # We define the possible classes for partial_fit
```

70

```python
        # In a real scenario, you might have more sophisticated
        ↪    labels
        self.classes_ = np.array([0, 1])  # 0: non-event, 1: event
        self.event_hashtag = event_hashtag

        # Buffer configuration
        self.tweet_texts = []
        self.labels = []
        self.batch_size = batch_size

    def on_status(self, status):
        """
        This method is called whenever a tweet is received.
        It parses the tweet, generates a label, and updates the NB
        ↪    model on-the-fly.
        """
        # Extract tweet text
        tweet_text = status.text

        # Basic cleaning
        cleaned_text = clean_tweet_text(tweet_text)

        # Simple labeling: if the tweet contains our "target"
        ↪    hashtag, label as event (1); else non-event (0)
        label = 1 if self.event_hashtag in cleaned_text else 0

        # Add to buffer
        self.tweet_texts.append(cleaned_text)
        self.labels.append(label)

        # If batch size reached, partial_fit on the model
        if len(self.tweet_texts) >= self.batch_size:
            self.partial_fit_model()

        return True

    def on_error(self, status_code):
        """
        If a non-200 status code is returned from Twitter, log or
        ↪    handle errors.
        """
        print(f"Encountered streaming error (status code:
        ↪    {status_code})")
        return False

    def partial_fit_model(self):
        """
        Vectorize the buffered tweets and partial_fit the Naive
        ↪    Bayes model on them.
        Then clear the buffer.
        """
        # Transform the buffered tweet texts into features
        X_new = self.vectorizer.transform(self.tweet_texts)
```

```python
        y_new = np.array(self.labels)

        # Apply partial_fit
        self.nb_classifier.partial_fit(X_new, y_new,
        ↪   classes=self.classes_)

        # Optionally print a quick sample classification report
        predictions = self.nb_classifier.predict(X_new)
        batch_accuracy = np.mean(predictions == y_new)
        print(f"Partial fit on batch of {len(X_new)}. Accuracy in
        ↪   this batch: {batch_accuracy:.2f}")

        # Clear buffers
        self.tweet_texts.clear()
        self.labels.clear()


########################################################################
# 4) Main logic: connect to Twitter, set up model, start streaming
########################################################################
def main():
    # Create and authenticate the Twitter API
    auth = tweepy.OAuthHandler(API_KEY, API_SECRET)
    auth.set_access_token(ACCESS_TOKEN, ACCESS_TOKEN_SECRET)
    api = tweepy.API(auth)

    # Initialize a CountVectorizer
    # In an online scenario, you might fit a large corpus or handle
    ↪   vocabulary updates
    # For demonstration we initialize an empty vocabulary and update
    ↪   it as tweets flow
    vectorizer = CountVectorizer(
        lowercase=True,
        stop_words='english',
        token_pattern=r'(?u)\b\w+\b'  # token pattern to keep
        ↪   meaningful words
    )

    # Initialize an empty vocabulary by "fitting" on a small dummy
    ↪   corpus
    dummy_corpus = ["dummy text"]
    vectorizer.fit(dummy_corpus)

    # Create the Naive Bayes classifier
    nb_classifier = MultinomialNB()

    # Perform an initial partial_fit with an empty or trivial batch
    ↪   to initialize class statistics
    X_init = vectorizer.transform(["dummy"])
    y_init = np.array([0])  # class 0
    nb_classifier.partial_fit(X_init, y_init, classes=np.array([0,
    ↪   1]))

    # Create a streaming listener
```

```python
# For demonstration, we choose "#disaster" as the "event" label
stream_listener = RealTimeTweetListener(nb_classifier,
↪    vectorizer, event_hashtag="#disaster", batch_size=5)

# Start filtering Twitter stream for some keywords or hashtags
# Adjust track terms for your use case
# NOTE: Twitter's streaming API might require elevated
↪    permissions for certain endpoints
stream = tweepy.Stream(auth=api.auth, listener=stream_listener)

try:
    # Filter by certain keywords, e.g. "disaster"
    print("Starting Twitter stream. Listening for tweets
↪    containing the word 'disaster'...")
    stream.filter(track=["disaster"], is_async=True)

    # In a real application, you might run indefinitely
    # Here, let's run for ~60 seconds then disconnect
    time.sleep(60)
    stream.disconnect()

except KeyboardInterrupt:
    # If user manually stops
    print("Keyboard interrupt received. Stopping stream.")
    stream.disconnect()

print("Finished streaming.")

if __name__ == "__main__":
    main()
```

Key Implementation Details:

- **Streaming Initialization:** We begin by authenticating via Tweepy and creating an instance of `RealTimeTweetListener` to process incoming data.

- **Preprocessing Tweets:** The `clean_tweet_text` function strips out URLs, mentions, and punctuation, and normalizes the text for vectorization.

- **Incremental Vectorization:** We use `CountVectorizer` to transform tweet texts into numerical feature vectors. In a large-scale application, you might dynamically update this vocabulary or use hashing-based vectorizers.

- **Naive Bayes Classifier:** We initialize `MultinomialNB` and use `partial_fit` to train on batches of streaming tweets.

The classifier is continuously refined as new labeled data arrives.

- **Label Assignment:** For illustration, we label tweets containing the target hashtag (e.g., #disaster) as an event (1) and all others as non-event (0). Real-world scenarios might involve more robust labeling or external annotation.

- **Batch Processing and Buffering:** Once enough tweets accumulate (based on the `batch_size`), the listener performs `partial_fit_model` to update the Naive Bayes model on those tweets, then clears the buffer for the next batch.

- **Handling Errors and Shutdown:** The `on_error` method manages any Twitter API errors, and the script stops gracefully after a set duration or upon keyboard interruption.

Chapter 15

Toxic Comment Classification

Online communities struggle with toxic or abusive comments. In this project, you will collect a dataset of comments accompanied by toxicity labels or severity scores. You will clean the text to remove markup, emojis, and profanity, then transform it with TF-IDF. A MultinomialNB classifier can be trained to detect and flag toxic comments automatically. Will walk you through creating training splits, fitting the model, and saving it for real-time comment scanning in a deployed setting.

- First, load a dataset (e.g., a CSV) containing user comments and associated toxicity labels.

- Clean each text entry by removing HTML tags and extraneous punctuation or emojis.

- Split the data into training and validation sets.

- Convert the cleaned text into numeric features using TF-IDF.

- Train a Naive Bayes classifier (MultinomialNB) on the transformed data.

- Evaluate accuracy and generate a classification report to examine precision, recall, and F1-score.

- Finally, save the model and vectorizer pipeline for real-time classification.

Python Code Snippet

```python
import re
import string
import pandas as pd
from sklearn.model_selection import train_test_split
from sklearn.feature_extraction.text import TfidfVectorizer
from sklearn.naive_bayes import MultinomialNB
from sklearn.metrics import classification_report, confusion_matrix,
↪   accuracy_score
import joblib

def clean_text(text):
    """
    Removes common HTML tags, punctuation, and excessive whitespace.
    This function can be extended to remove or handle emojis and
    ↪   other
    undesired tokens for further cleaning.
    """
    # Remove HTML tags
    text = re.sub(r'<.*?>', '', text)
    # Remove punctuation
    text = text.translate(str.maketrans('', '', string.punctuation))
    # Convert to lowercase
    text = text.lower()
    # Remove extra whitespace
    text = re.sub(r'\s+', ' ', text).strip()
    return text

def main():
    # ------------------------------------------------------------
    # 1) Load dataset (CSV of comments & labels)
    # ------------------------------------------------------------
    # Suppose 'data/toxic_comments.csv' has two columns:
    # 'comment_text' and 'toxic_label' (0=not toxic, 1=toxic)
    df = pd.read_csv('data/toxic_comments.csv')

    # ------------------------------------------------------------
    # 2) Clean text
    # ------------------------------------------------------------
    df['cleaned_text'] = df['comment_text'].apply(clean_text)

    # ------------------------------------------------------------
    # 3) Split data into train and test
    # ------------------------------------------------------------
    X = df['cleaned_text'].values
    y = df['toxic_label'].values

    X_train, X_test, y_train, y_test = train_test_split(
        X, y, test_size=0.2, random_state=42, stratify=y
    )
```

```
# ------------------------------------------------------------
# 4) Convert text into TF-IDF features
# ------------------------------------------------------------
# Initialize the TF-IDF Vectorizer
tfidf = TfidfVectorizer(
    max_features=5000,  # limit to 5000 features for
    ↪  demonstration
    ngram_range=(1, 2), # use unigrams and bigrams
    stop_words='english'
)

# Fit on training data only, then transform both train and test
X_train_tfidf = tfidf.fit_transform(X_train)
X_test_tfidf = tfidf.transform(X_test)

    # ------------------------------------------------------------
    # 5) Train a Multinomial Naive Bayes model
    # ------------------------------------------------------------
    model = MultinomialNB(alpha=1.0)
    model.fit(X_train_tfidf, y_train)

    # ------------------------------------------------------------
    # 6) Evaluate performance on test set
    # ------------------------------------------------------------
    y_pred = model.predict(X_test_tfidf)

    # Print metrics
    print("Accuracy:", accuracy_score(y_test, y_pred))
    print("\nClassification Report:")
    print(classification_report(y_test, y_pred))
    print("\nConfusion Matrix:")
    print(confusion_matrix(y_test, y_pred))

    # ------------------------------------------------------------
    # 7) Save model and TF-IDF vectorizer
    # ------------------------------------------------------------
    # This can be used for real-time or later offline inference
    joblib.dump(model, 'naive_bayes_toxic_model.joblib')
    joblib.dump(tfidf, 'tfidf_vectorizer.joblib')
    print("\nModel and vectorizer saved successfully.")

if __name__ == "__main__":
    main()
```

Key Implementation Details:

- **Data Cleaning:** The `clean_text` function filters out HTML tags, punctuation, and extra whitespace. Additional steps (e.g., handling emojis or special characters) can be easily included.

- **Train-Test Split:** By using the `train_test_split` approach with a fixed random state, reproducible results allow for consistent evaluation of the `MultinomialNB` classifier's performance.

- **TF-IDF Vectorization:** The `TfidfVectorizer` converts text into numerical features, emphasizing distinguishing terms over frequently appearing ones. Here, we limit to 5000 features for demonstration.

- **Naive Bayes Training:** We employ `MultinomialNB`, a common choice for text classification due to its effectiveness on TF-IDF or count-based features. The smoothing parameter (`alpha`) can be tuned if needed.

- **Evaluation Metrics:** We rely on `accuracy_score`, `classification_report`, and a `confusion_matrix` to understand how effectively toxic vs. non-toxic comments are classified.

- **Model Saving:** Finally, the trained `MultinomialNB` model and `TfidfVectorizer` are stored using `joblib` for convenient real-time inference in a deployed environment.

Chapter 16

Building a Simple Naive Bayes Recommender System

Here, you will explore how Naive Bayes can be adapted for recommendation tasks. The approach focuses on modeling the likelihood that a user might prefer a product or item based on the user's historical interactions or attribute data. You will store user-item interactions in a structured format, convert them to a set of features (e.g., item category, user demographics, usage frequency), and train a Bernoulli NB model to predict interest. Python examples will detail data wrangling, encoding strategies, and how to generate ranked recommendations.

- First, collect or synthesize a dataset containing user attributes (age, gender, etc.), item attributes (category, price range, etc.), and historical user-item interactions (clicks, purchases, etc.).

- Convert these raw attributes into binary, categorical, or numeric features suitable for Bernoulli Naive Bayes.

- Split the data into training and test sets to evaluate the model's predictive performance.

- Train a Bernoulli Naive Bayes classifier that estimates the probability of a user expressing interest in a given item.

- Finally, use predicted probabilities to generate a ranked list of recommended items for each user.

Python Code Snippet

```python
import numpy as np
import pandas as pd
from sklearn.model_selection import train_test_split
from sklearn.naive_bayes import BernoulliNB
from sklearn.preprocessing import LabelBinarizer
from sklearn.metrics import accuracy_score, classification_report

def generate_synthetic_data():
    """
    Generates a small synthetic dataset for demonstration.
    Returns:
        user_df (pd.DataFrame): Table of user features
        item_df (pd.DataFrame): Table of item features
        interactions_df (pd.DataFrame): Table of user-item
        ↪    interactions
    """
    # Example user data
    user_data = {
        'user_id': [1, 2, 3, 4, 5],
        'age': [23, 45, 31, 22, 55],
        'gender': ['F', 'M', 'M', 'F', 'F']
    }
    user_df = pd.DataFrame(user_data)

    # Example item data
    item_data = {
        'item_id': [101, 102, 103, 104, 105, 106],
        'category': ['Books', 'Books', 'Electronics', 'Electronics',
        ↪    'Clothing', 'Clothing'],
        'price_range': ['low', 'medium', 'high', 'medium', 'low',
        ↪    'low']
    }
    item_df = pd.DataFrame(item_data)

    # Synthetic user-item interactions (1 = user showed interest, 0
    ↪    = no interest)
    # For simplicity, assume each user has some pattern of interest
    interactions_data = {
        'user_id': [1, 1, 2, 2, 3, 3, 4, 4, 4, 5, 5],
        'item_id': [101, 102, 101, 104, 103, 105, 102, 103, 106,
        ↪    101, 105],
        'interest': [1, 0, 1, 1, 1, 1, 0, 1, 1, 1, 0]
    }
    interactions_df = pd.DataFrame(interactions_data)
```

```python
    return user_df, item_df, interactions_df

def merge_datasets(user_df, item_df, interactions_df):
    """
    Merges user, item, and interaction data into one DataFrame
    ↪  suitable for modeling.
    Returns:
      merged_df (pd.DataFrame): Contains columns for user features,
      ↪  item features, and interest label.
    """
    # Merge user features into interactions
    temp_df = pd.merge(interactions_df, user_df, on='user_id',
    ↪  how='left')

    # Merge item features
    merged_df = pd.merge(temp_df, item_df, on='item_id', how='left')
    # Columns: user_id, item_id, interest, age, gender, category,
    ↪  price_range
    return merged_df

def encode_features(df):
    """
    Encodes categorical features into binary indicators suitable for
    ↪  Bernoulli Naive Bayes.
    Returns:
      X (np.ndarray): Feature array
      y (np.ndarray): Binary interest array
      feature_names (list): List of feature column names after
      ↪  encoding
    """
    # Separate label from features
    y = df['interest'].values

    # We'll encode user_id and item_id as well,
    # though in a real scenario we might handle them differently
    ↪  (e.g., embeddings).
    feature_cols = ['user_id', 'item_id', 'age', 'gender',
    ↪  'category', 'price_range']
    raw_features = df[feature_cols].copy()

    # Convert numerical columns to float or int
    raw_features['age'] = raw_features['age'].astype(float)

    # Use LabelBinarizer for each categorical column
    lb = LabelBinarizer()

    # We'll collect the encoded frames in a list
    encoded_arrays = []
    feature_names = []

    for col in raw_features.columns:
        if raw_features[col].dtype == object:  # categorical
            # Fit the label-binarizer if needed
```

```
            encoded = lb.fit_transform(raw_features[col])
            # Build column names
            binarized_col_names = [f"{col}_{cls}" for cls in
            ↪    lb.classes_]
            encoded_arrays.append(encoded)
            feature_names.extend(binarized_col_names)
        else:  # numeric
            # Reshape needed to feed into .fit_transform if we used
            ↪    LabelBinarizer
            # But for numeric columns, we can directly add them to
            ↪    the final X

            ↪    encoded_arrays.append(raw_features[col].values.reshape(-1,
            ↪    1))
            feature_names.append(col)

    # Concatenate all feature columns
    X = np.hstack(encoded_arrays)
    return X, y, feature_names

def train_naive_bayes(X_train, y_train):
    """
    Trains a Bernoulli Naive Bayes classifier.
    Returns:
      model (BernoulliNB): Trained BernoulliNB model
    """
    model = BernoulliNB()
    model.fit(X_train, y_train)
    return model

def evaluate_model(model, X_test, y_test):
    """
    Evaluates the model on test data, prints accuracy and
    ↪    classification report.
    """
    y_pred = model.predict(X_test)
    acc = accuracy_score(y_test, y_pred)
    print(f"Test Accuracy: {acc:.4f}")
    print("Classification Report:")
    print(classification_report(y_test, y_pred, zero_division=0))

def recommend_items_for_user(model, feature_names, df, user_id,
↪    all_items, top_n=3):
    """
    Generates item recommendations for a specific user based on the
    ↪    learned model.
    We compute the probability of interest for each item not yet in
    ↪    user history.
    Args:
      model (BernoulliNB): Trained model
      feature_names (list): List of encoded feature names
      df (pd.DataFrame): Original merged dataset with user/item
      ↪    features
```

```python
    user_id (int): Target user to recommend items to
    all_items (pd.DataFrame): Reference table of all items
    top_n (int): Number of top recommendations to return
    """
    # Collect user features from the first row matching user_id
    user_row = df[df['user_id'] == user_id].iloc[0]
    user_age = user_row['age']
    user_gender = user_row['gender']

    # Identify which items user already has an interaction record
    ↪   for
    user_items = df[df['user_id'] == user_id]['item_id'].unique()
    candidate_items =
    ↪   all_items[~all_items['item_id'].isin(user_items)]

    predictions = []
    for _, item_row in candidate_items.iterrows():
        # Create a single row DataFrame to encode
        temporary_df = pd.DataFrame([{
            'user_id': user_id,
            'item_id': item_row['item_id'],
            'age': user_age,
            'gender': user_gender,
            'category': item_row['category'],
            'price_range': item_row['price_range']
        }])

        # Encode it
        X_temp, _, _ = encode_features(temporary_df)
        # Predict probability of interest
        prob = model.predict_proba(X_temp)[0][1]   # Probability for
        ↪   class '1'
        predictions.append((item_row['item_id'], prob))

    # Sort candidate items by highest predicted probability
    predictions.sort(key=lambda x: x[1], reverse=True)
    recommended = predictions[:top_n]
    print(f"Top {top_n} Recommended items for User {user_id}:")
    for item_id, score in recommended:
        print(f"  Item {item_id} with predicted interest probability
        ↪   {score:.4f}")

def main():
    print("=== Generating Synthetic Data ===")
    user_df, item_df, interactions_df = generate_synthetic_data()

    print("\n=== Merging Datasets ===")
    merged_df = merge_datasets(user_df, item_df, interactions_df)

    print("\n=== Encoding Features ===")
    X, y, feature_names = encode_features(merged_df)

    print("\n=== Splitting into Train/Test ===")
```

```
X_train, X_test, y_train, y_test = train_test_split(
    X, y, test_size=0.3, random_state=42
)

print("\n=== Training Bernoulli Naive Bayes Model ===")
model = train_naive_bayes(X_train, y_train)

print("\n=== Evaluating Model ===")
evaluate_model(model, X_test, y_test)

print("\n=== Generating Sample Recommendations ===")
# Recommend for user_id=1
recommend_items_for_user(
    model, feature_names, merged_df, user_id=1,
    ↪  all_items=item_df, top_n=3
)

# Recommend for user_id=5
recommend_items_for_user(
    model, feature_names, merged_df, user_id=5,
    ↪  all_items=item_df, top_n=3
)

if __name__ == "__main__":
    main()
```

Key Implementation Details:

- **Data Merging and Cleaning:** We consolidate user attributes, item attributes, and interactions into a single dataset using `merge_datasets`.

- **Feature Encoding:** The helper `encode_features` applies `LabelBinarizer` to categorical fields, converting them into binary indicators for Bernoulli Naive Bayes.

- **Model Training:** We use `BernoulliNB` from scikit-learn and fit it via `train_naive_bayes`.

- **Evaluation:** Accuracy and other metrics are computed using `accuracy_score` and `classification_report` to gauge model performance.

- **Recommendations:** `recommend_items_for_user` predicts the probability of user interest for items not yet interacted with, then ranks and returns the top items.

Chapter 17

Multi-class Email Categorization

Beyond spam/ham filtering, email can be organized into multiple categories such as promotions, personal, work, social, or updates. You will learn to construct a multi-class Naive Bayes classifier by preparing a labeled training set with these category labels. The workflow involves text cleaning, tokenization, vectorization, and training with MultinomialNB, which naturally supports multiple classes. Will illustrate how to produce confusion matrices for each category, helping you refine the feature set and classification approach.

- First, prepare a labeled dataset with multiple email categories (e.g., promotions, personal, work, social, updates).

- Next, clean and tokenize the text to remove noise such as punctuation or extra spaces, then transform it into numeric features (TF-IDF or frequency counts).

- Instantiate and train a Multinomial Naive Bayes classifier, which naturally supports multi-class problems.

- Finally, evaluate performance using a confusion matrix and metrics such as precision, recall, and F1-scores for each category.

Python Code Snippet

```python
import re
import string
import numpy as np
from sklearn.feature_extraction.text import TfidfVectorizer
from sklearn.model_selection import train_test_split
from sklearn.naive_bayes import MultinomialNB
from sklearn.metrics import confusion_matrix, classification_report
import itertools
import matplotlib.pyplot as plt

def clean_text(raw_text):
    """
    Basic text cleaning function that lowercases the text, removes
    ↪   punctuation
    and multiple spaces, etc.
    """
    # Lowercase
    text = raw_text.lower()
    # Remove punctuation using str.translate
    text = text.translate(str.maketrans('', '', string.punctuation))
    # Remove extra spaces
    text = re.sub(r'\s+', ' ', text).strip()
    return text

def plot_confusion_matrix(cm, classes, title='Confusion matrix',
    ↪   cmap=plt.cm.Blues):
    """
    Utility function to plot a confusion matrix using matplotlib.
    """
    plt.imshow(cm, interpolation='nearest', cmap=cmap)
    plt.title(title)
    plt.colorbar()
    tick_marks = np.arange(len(classes))
    plt.xticks(tick_marks, classes, rotation=45)
    plt.yticks(tick_marks, classes)

    # Print confusion matrix values inside each cell
    thresh = cm.max() / 2.
    for i, j in itertools.product(range(cm.shape[0]),
    ↪   range(cm.shape[1])):
        plt.text(j, i, cm[i, j],
                horizontalalignment="center",
                color="white" if cm[i, j] > thresh else "black")

    plt.tight_layout()
    plt.ylabel('True label')
    plt.xlabel('Predicted label')

def main():
    """
```

```
Main function to demonstrate multi-class email categorization
↪  using
a Naive Bayes classifier. This script:

1) Defines a small dataset of sample emails with various
↪  categories.
2) Cleans and vectorizes the text with TfidfVectorizer.
3) Trains a MultinomialNB model on the training set.
4) Evaluates the model using confusion matrices and
↪  classification reports.
5) Plots and saves the confusion matrix.
"""
# Sample data: each entry is (email_text, category)
# Categories: 'personal', 'promotions', 'work', 'social',
↪  'updates'
data_samples = [
    ("Hey, are we still on for dinner tonight? Let me know!",
    ↪  "personal"),
    ("Limited-time offer! 50% off your next purchase of shoes!",
    ↪  "promotions"),
    ("Project Meeting is scheduled for Monday morning. Bring
    ↪  reports.", "work"),
    ("Don't forget to wish Sarah a happy birthday via
    ↪  Facebook!", "social"),
    ("Your account has been updated with the latest security
    ↪  patches.", "updates"),
    ("Family reunion on Sunday! Let's plan the potluck items in
    ↪  detail.", "personal"),
    ("Big Sale this weekend only: buy 1 get 1 free on selected
    ↪  items!", "promotions"),
    ("Reminder: Quarterly review documents must be submitted by
    ↪  Friday.", "work"),
    ("Check out this new social group for local sports events.",
    ↪  "social"),
    ("Your billing statement is ready for review.", "updates"),
    ("Just finished my training session, feeling great!",
    ↪  "personal"),
    ("Special discount for new members, join now and save big.",
    ↪  "promotions"),
    ("Weekly team sync has been moved to Thursday. Mark your
    ↪  calendar.", "work"),
    ("Join our Slack channel to connect with your friends
    ↪  instantly!", "social"),
    ("System maintenance scheduled tomorrow, you may experience
    ↪  minor downtime.", "updates"),
]

# Separate texts and labels
texts = [sample[0] for sample in data_samples]
labels = [sample[1] for sample in data_samples]

# Clean the text
cleaned_texts = [clean_text(t) for t in texts]
```

```python
# Create TF-IDF features
vectorizer = TfidfVectorizer(stop_words='english')
X = vectorizer.fit_transform(cleaned_texts)  # Feature matrix
y = np.array(labels)

# Split into train and test sets
X_train, X_test, y_train, y_test = train_test_split(
    X, y, test_size=0.3, random_state=42, stratify=labels
)

# Instantiate MultinomialNB
nb_model = MultinomialNB()

# Train the Naive Bayes model
nb_model.fit(X_train, y_train)

# Predict on test set
y_pred = nb_model.predict(X_test)

# Evaluate model
print("Classification Report:")
print(classification_report(y_test, y_pred))

# Confusion matrix
cm = confusion_matrix(y_test, y_pred)
category_names = sorted(list(set(labels)))
print("Confusion Matrix (Raw):")
print(cm)

# Plot confusion matrix
plt.figure(figsize=(6, 6))
plot_confusion_matrix(cm, classes=category_names,
                      title='Multi-class Email Categorization
                      ↪ Confusion Matrix')
plt.savefig("confusion_matrix.png")
plt.show()

# Demonstrate using the model for a new "unseen" email
new_emails = [
    "Flash Sale: Earn double rewards on all stationery products
    ↪ this week only!",
    "Dad, can you pick me up at the airport on Saturday
    ↪ afternoon?"
]
cleaned_new = [clean_text(n) for n in new_emails]
new_features = vectorizer.transform(cleaned_new)
new_preds = nb_model.predict(new_features)

print("\nSample Predictions on New Emails:")
for email_text, pred_label in zip(new_emails, new_preds):
    print(f"Email: '{email_text}' => Predicted Category:
    ↪ {pred_label}")
```

```
if __name__ == "__main__":
    main()
```

Key Implementation Details:

- **Data Preparation:** We create a small labeled dataset where each sample is an email text with a corresponding category among promotions, personal, work, social, or updates.

- **Text Cleaning:** A custom `clean_text` function lowercases the text, removes punctuation, and condenses multiple spaces.

- **Feature Extraction:** `TfidfVectorizer` converts the cleaned emails into TF-IDF features, which capture term frequency and downweight common words.

- **Naive Bayes Model:** We instantiate `MultinomialNB` from scikit-learn and fit on the training portion of our dataset. This variant of Naive Bayes works well for text data represented as counts or TF-IDF scores.

- **Evaluation Metrics:** We compute a confusion matrix and a detailed classification report to understand misclassifications among multiple categories. The `plot_confusion_matrix` function creates a heatmap for more intuitive visualization.

- **Prediction on Unseen Data:** With `textttpredict`, we show how to classify new examples by processing them through the same cleaning and vectorization steps.

Chapter 18

Multi-label Tagging of Documents and Articles

In some scenarios, a document may belong to more than one category or have multiple applicable tags. This chapter delves into multi-label classification with Naive Bayes. You will learn to set up a one-vs-rest architecture for each label, then train separate NB models for each tag. Will show how to transform labels into a multi-hot vector representation, streamline training with scikit-learn's multi-label utilities, and generate multiple predictions per document.

- We begin by preparing a sample dataset of documents, each associated with multiple labels.

- Next, we use `MultiLabelBinarizer` to convert each set of labels into a multi-hot vector.

- We vectorize the text data (e.g., using TF-IDF).

- We train a Naive Bayes model for each label through the `OneVsRestClassifier` wrapper.

- Finally, we evaluate performance, observing how many relevant tags the model can correctly predict.

Python Code Snippet

```python
import numpy as np
from sklearn.feature_extraction.text import TfidfVectorizer
from sklearn.preprocessing import MultiLabelBinarizer
from sklearn.model_selection import train_test_split
from sklearn.naive_bayes import MultinomialNB
from sklearn.multiclass import OneVsRestClassifier
from sklearn.metrics import classification_report

def create_example_dataset():
    """
    Creates a small example dataset with documents
    and a list of their associated labels.
    Returns:
        documents (list of str): Text documents.
        labels (list of list of str): List of label lists.
    """
    documents = [
        "I love reading about AI and machine learning",
        "My cat loves fish and chicken",
        "The dog plays in the park",
        "Deep learning and neural networks are fascinating",
        "I enjoy a good steak for dinner",
        "Neural networks can perform image recognition tasks",
        "Graphical models and Bayesian networks are related",
        "He bakes the best homemade bread",
        "AI research has led to breakthroughs in healthcare",
        "I take my dog for a walk every morning"
    ]

    labels = [
        ["technology", "ai"],
        ["pets"],
        ["pets"],
        ["technology", "ai"],
        ["food"],
        ["technology", "ai"],
        ["technology"],
        ["food"],
        ["technology", "ai"],
        ["pets"]
    ]
    return documents, labels

def vectorize_text(documents):
    """
    Uses TF-IDF to vectorize the list of documents.
    Returns:
        vectorizer (TfidfVectorizer): Fitted TF-IDF vectorizer.
        X (sparse matrix): TF-IDF feature matrix for the documents.
    """
```

```python
    vectorizer = TfidfVectorizer(stop_words='english')
    X = vectorizer.fit_transform(documents)
    return vectorizer, X

def binarize_labels(labels):
    """
    Convert a list of label lists into multi-hot (binary) vectors
    using MultiLabelBinarizer.
    Returns:
        mlb (MultiLabelBinarizer): Fitted binarizer.
        Y (ndarray): Binary label matrix.
    """
    mlb = MultiLabelBinarizer()
    Y = mlb.fit_transform(labels)
    return mlb, Y

def train_and_evaluate_naive_bayes(X_train, Y_train, X_test, Y_test,
    mlb):
    """
    Train a OneVsRestClassifier with MultinomialNB for multi-label
        classification.
    Print classification report on the test set.
    """
    # OneVsRestClassifier trains a separate model per label
    clf = OneVsRestClassifier(MultinomialNB(alpha=1.0))
    clf.fit(X_train, Y_train)

    # Predict on test data
    Y_pred = clf.predict(X_test)

    # Convert predictions back to label sets for demonstration
    predicted_label_sets = mlb.inverse_transform(Y_pred)

    print("Predicted labels for test documents:")
    for i, plabels in enumerate(predicted_label_sets):
        print(f"Document {i+1}: {plabels}")

    # Evaluate
    print("\nClassification Report (per label):")
    print(classification_report(Y_test, Y_pred,
        target_names=mlb.classes_, zero_division=0))

def main():
    # 1) Create dataset
    documents, labels = create_example_dataset()

    # 2) Vectorize documents
    vectorizer, X = vectorize_text(documents)

    # 3) Binarize labels
    mlb, Y = binarize_labels(labels)

    # Split into train/test
```

```
X_train, X_test, Y_train, Y_test = train_test_split(
    X, Y, test_size=0.3, random_state=42
)

# 4) Train and evaluate
train_and_evaluate_naive_bayes(X_train, Y_train, X_test, Y_test,
↪  mlb)

if __name__ == "__main__":
    main()
```

Key Implementation Details:

- **Dataset Creation:** We generate a small sample dataset in `create_example_dataset`, returning documents and their associated lists of labels.

- **Vectorization:** The `vectorize_text` function applies TF-IDF to convert raw text documents into numerical feature vectors suitable for training.

- **MultiLabelBinarizer:** We apply `binarize_labels` to produce a binary matrix of labels. Each column corresponds to one possible label.

- **Naive Bayes Classification:** Using `OneVsRestClassifier(MultinomialNB(...))`, we train separate Multinomial Naive Bayes classifiers for each label. This is the essence of the one-vs-rest approach for multi-label tasks.

- **Evaluation:** In `train_and_evaluate_naive_bayes`, we predict which tags each test document belongs to and print a classification report, detailing precision and recall on a per-label basis.

Chapter 19

Comparing Multinomial and Bernoulli Naive Bayes for Text Classification

With text tasks, both MultinomialNB and BernoulliNB can be used, but each excels in different situations. You will build parallel pipelines using scikit-learn, applying both models to the same dataset (e.g., movie reviews or product comments). The chapter provides Python code to compare how the two variants handle feature representations such as term frequencies vs. binary presence indicators. Through hands-on examples, you will learn to interpret performance variations and choose the appropriate NB variant for a given text classification challenge.

- Load a labeled text dataset—in the following example, we use `fetch_20newsgroups` from scikit-learn to demonstrate multi-category classification.

- Define two parallel pipelines—one uses MultinomialNB with term-count or TF-IDF features; the other uses BernoulliNB with binary presence features.

- Fit each pipeline on the training set and evaluate on the test set, comparing accuracy and other relevant metrics like the confusion matrix or classification report.

- Explore how the different variants of Naive Bayes perform on texts of varying lengths and language complexity, and interpret which model best handles specific text classification tasks.

Python Code Snippet

```python
import numpy as np
from sklearn.datasets import fetch_20newsgroups
from sklearn.model_selection import train_test_split
from sklearn.feature_extraction.text import CountVectorizer,
↪   TfidfVectorizer
from sklearn.naive_bayes import MultinomialNB, BernoulliNB
from sklearn.pipeline import Pipeline
from sklearn.metrics import accuracy_score, classification_report,
↪   confusion_matrix

def train_and_evaluate_model(model_pipeline, X_train, y_train,
↪   X_test, y_test, model_name="NB"):
    """
    Trains the model pipeline on (X_train, y_train) and evaluates on
    ↪   (X_test, y_test).
    Prints the accuracy, confusion matrix, and classification
    ↪   report.
    """
    print(f"Training and evaluating {model_name}...")
    model_pipeline.fit(X_train, y_train)
    predictions = model_pipeline.predict(X_test)

    acc = accuracy_score(y_test, predictions)
    print(f"Accuracy for {model_name}: {acc:.4f}")
    print("Confusion Matrix:")
    print(confusion_matrix(y_test, predictions))
    print("Classification Report:")
    print(classification_report(y_test, predictions))

def main():
    # 1) Load data from scikit-learn's 20 Newsgroups dataset
    #    We choose a subset of categories for brevity
    categories = [
        'comp.graphics',
        'rec.sport.hockey',
        'talk.politics.mideast',
        'soc.religion.christian'
    ]
    newsgroups_train = fetch_20newsgroups(subset='train',
    ↪   categories=categories, shuffle=True, random_state=42)
    newsgroups_test = fetch_20newsgroups(subset='test',
    ↪   categories=categories, shuffle=True, random_state=42)
```

95

```
X_train, y_train = newsgroups_train.data,
↪   newsgroups_train.target
X_test, y_test = newsgroups_test.data, newsgroups_test.target

# 2) Define parallel pipelines for MultinomialNB and BernoulliNB
#    Using TF-IDF or CountVectorizer to illustrate difference

# Pipeline A: MultinomialNB with TF-IDF
multinomial_pipeline = Pipeline([
    ('tfidf', TfidfVectorizer()),
    ('clf', MultinomialNB())
])

# Pipeline B: BernoulliNB with binary (presence/absence)
↪   features
bernoulli_pipeline = Pipeline([
    ('count_bin', CountVectorizer(binary=True)),
    ('clf', BernoulliNB())
])

# 3) Train and evaluate the two pipelines
train_and_evaluate_model(multinomial_pipeline, X_train, y_train,
↪   X_test, y_test, model_name="MultinomialNB with TF-IDF")
train_and_evaluate_model(bernoulli_pipeline, X_train, y_train,
↪   X_test, y_test, model_name="BernoulliNB with Binary
↪   Features")

if __name__ == '__main__':
    main()
```

Key Implementation Details:

- **Dataset Loading:** We use 20 Newsgroups data, which provides text-based samples from multiple topical categories.

- **Data Representation:** MultinomialNB generally operates on counts (or TF-IDF). In this snippet, we apply `TfidfVectorizer` to demonstrate frequency-based weighting for the MultinomialNB pipeline. Conversely, BernoulliNB readily handles binary features, so `CountVectorizer` is configured with `binary=True`.

- **Pipelines:** Both pipelines encapsulate feature extraction and classifier instantiation. This modular design simplifies the comparison of different `Vectorizer` or `Naive Bayes` variants.

- **Training and Evaluation:** The function `train_and_evaluate_model` trains the pipeline using the train-

96

ing set, then prints accuracy, a confusion matrix, and a classification report to reflect model performance on the test set.

- **Model Variants for Text:** MultinomialNB is often favored for TF-IDF or raw term counts, while BernoulliNB can excel when text presence/absence (binary features) is crucial, especially for shorter texts or scenarios where term frequency magnitudes are less relevant.

Chapter 20

Leveraging Gaussian Naive Bayes for Continuous Data

This chapter shows how GaussianNB can be utilized for tasks where features are measured on continuous scales. You will explore a dataset containing continuous attributes, such as sensor readings or geographic data. The code examples walk through verifying assumptions about feature distributions, applying transformations (e.g., log-scaling), and training the classifier. The Python workflow highlights how to handle outliers and evaluate predictive accuracy when dealing with real-valued inputs.

- Generate or load a dataset with continuous features.

- Optionally detect and address outliers (e.g., above a z-score threshold).

- Apply transformations, such as log-scaling, to normalize skewed variables.

- Train a GaussianNB classifier, focusing on how it models continuous data via normal (Gaussian) assumptions.

- Evaluate predictive accuracy with test data.

Python Code Snippet

```python
import numpy as np
import pandas as pd
from sklearn.naive_bayes import GaussianNB
from sklearn.model_selection import train_test_split
from sklearn.preprocessing import StandardScaler
from sklearn.metrics import accuracy_score, classification_report
import scipy.stats as stats

def generate_synthetic_data(num_samples=500, random_seed=42):
    """
    Generate a synthetic dataset with continuous features and binary
    ↪    labels.
    Features:
      - temperature: around a normal distribution
      - pressure: around a normal distribution, with optional offset
      - humidity: another continuous feature
    Labels:
      - 0 or 1 based on a threshold that combines these features
    """
    np.random.seed(random_seed)

    # For demonstration, let's create normally distributed features
    temperature = np.random.normal(loc=25.0, scale=5.0,
    ↪    size=num_samples)  # e.g., degrees Celsius
    pressure = np.random.normal(loc=1013.0, scale=10.0,
    ↪    size=num_samples) # hPa
    humidity = np.random.normal(loc=60.0, scale=15.0,
    ↪    size=num_samples)   # percent

    # Combine them into a single array
    X = np.column_stack((temperature, pressure, humidity))

    # Define a label based on an arbitrary condition:
    #    If (temp - 25) + 0.01*(pressure - 1013) + 0.1*(humidity -
    ↪    60) > 0 => label 1 else 0
    conditions = ( (temperature - 25) + 0.01 * (pressure - 1013) +
    ↪    0.1 * (humidity - 60) )
    y = (conditions > 0).astype(int)

    return X, y

def remove_outliers_zscore(X, y, threshold=3.0):
    """
    Remove outliers from dataset using a z-score threshold.
    Returns trimmed X and y.
    """
    z_scores = np.abs(stats.zscore(X))
    # We combine over all features; keep only rows where all
    ↪    features are below threshold
    mask = (z_scores < threshold).all(axis=1)
```

```python
    X_clean, y_clean = X[mask], y[mask]
    return X_clean, y_clean

def apply_log_transform_to_positive_features(X,
↪   feature_indices=None):
    """
    Log-transform the selected feature indices in X.
    Only apply if the values are strictly positive.
    """
    if feature_indices is None:
        feature_indices = []

    X_transformed = np.copy(X)
    for idx in feature_indices:
        # Ensure positivity by checking min
        min_value = np.min(X_transformed[:, idx])
        if min_value <= 0:
            # Shift data so that everything is > 0
            shift_amount = np.abs(min_value) + 1e-9
            X_transformed[:, idx] += shift_amount
        # Apply log transform
        X_transformed[:, idx] = np.log(X_transformed[:, idx])

    return X_transformed

def train_gaussian_nb_classifier(X_train, y_train):
    """
    Train a Gaussian Naive Bayes model on the given data.
    """
    model = GaussianNB()
    model.fit(X_train, y_train)
    return model

def evaluate_model_performance(model, X_test, y_test):
    """
    Evaluate the trained model on test data and print metrics.
    """
    y_pred = model.predict(X_test)
    acc = accuracy_score(y_test, y_pred)
    print("Accuracy on test set:", acc)
    print("\nClassification Report:")
    print(classification_report(y_test, y_pred))

def main():
    # 1) Generate synthetic data
    X, y = generate_synthetic_data(num_samples=500, random_seed=42)

    # 2) (Optional) Remove outliers using z-score approach
    X_clean, y_clean = remove_outliers_zscore(X, y, threshold=3.0)

    # 3) Apply log transform to chosen features if needed
    #    Suppose we log-transform the 'humidity' (index 2) if we
↪    suspect it's skewed
```

100

```
X_transformed =
↪  apply_log_transform_to_positive_features(X_clean,
↪  feature_indices=[2])

# 4) Scale features to meet typical classifier assumptions
scaler = StandardScaler()
X_scaled = scaler.fit_transform(X_transformed)

# 5) Train-test split
X_train, X_test, y_train, y_test = train_test_split(
    X_scaled, y_clean, test_size=0.2, random_state=42
)

# 6) Train the Gaussian Naive Bayes classifier
model = train_gaussian_nb_classifier(X_train, y_train)

# 7) Evaluate performance
evaluate_model_performance(model, X_test, y_test)

if __name__ == "__main__":
    main()
```

Key Implementation Details:

- **Data Generation:** We synthesize continuous-valued features (e.g., temperature, pressure, humidity) to mimic real-world sensor data, then derive binary labels with a simple condition.

- **Outlier Handling:** The function `remove_outliers_zscore` uses a z-score threshold to discard rows that deviate significantly from the mean, helping the GaussianNB model better fit typical data points.

- **Feature Transformations:** We selectively apply a log transform to positive features via `apply_log_transform_to_positive_features` if distributions are skewed. Shifts are added if any values are non-positive.

- **Model Training:** The `train_gaussian_nb_classifier` routine trains a `GaussianNB` model, which fits a normal distribution to each feature per class.

- **Evaluation:** Using the held-out test set, `evaluate_model_performance` reports accuracy and a detailed classification report, guiding further tuning and transformation steps.

Chapter 21

Feature Selection Methods for Naive Bayes

Sometimes, the presence of irrelevant or redundant features can degrade NB performance. You will learn techniques like univariate selection, mutual information, and recursive feature elimination to isolate the most informative features for a Naive Bayes model. The Python code will illustrate each technique, showing how to prune feature sets and measure the subsequent impact on classification performance. Detailed steps include adjusting parameters for feature selection methods, identifying optimal subsets, and training the refined model.

Python Code Snippet

```
import numpy as np
import random
import warnings

from sklearn.datasets import make_classification
from sklearn.model_selection import train_test_split,
↪   cross_val_score
from sklearn.feature_selection import SelectKBest, f_classif,
↪   mutual_info_classif, RFE
from sklearn.naive_bayes import GaussianNB
from sklearn.metrics import accuracy_score
```

```python
from sklearn.pipeline import Pipeline

warnings.filterwarnings('ignore')

def set_seed(seed=42):
    """
    Set the random seed for reproducibility.
    """
    random.seed(seed)
    np.random.seed(seed)

def demonstrate_univariate_selection(X_train, X_test, y_train,
↪  y_test, k=10):
    """
    Demonstrates univariate feature selection using SelectKBest
    ↪  (f_classif).
    Returns the accuracy on the test set after training a Naive
    ↪  Bayes model.
    """
    # Create a pipeline that first selects top k features with
    ↪  f_classif, then fits a GaussianNB
    pipe = Pipeline([
        ('select_k_best', SelectKBest(score_func=f_classif, k=k)),
        ('nb_model', GaussianNB())
    ])
    pipe.fit(X_train, y_train)
    y_pred = pipe.predict(X_test)
    return accuracy_score(y_test, y_pred)

def demonstrate_mutual_information(X_train, X_test, y_train, y_test,
↪  k=10):
    """
    Demonstrates feature selection using SelectKBest
    ↪  (mutual_info_classif).
    Returns the accuracy on the test set after training a Naive
    ↪  Bayes model.
    """
    # Create a pipeline that first selects top k features with
    ↪  mutual_info_classif, then fits a GaussianNB
    pipe = Pipeline([
        ('select_k_best',
        ↪  SelectKBest(score_func=mutual_info_classif, k=k)),
        ('nb_model', GaussianNB())
    ])
    pipe.fit(X_train, y_train)
    y_pred = pipe.predict(X_test)
    return accuracy_score(y_test, y_pred)

def demonstrate_rfe(X_train, X_test, y_train, y_test,
↪  n_features=10):
    """
    Demonstrates Recursive Feature Elimination (RFE) using a Naive
    ↪  Bayes model.
```

```python
    Returns the accuracy on the test set after training a Naive
    ↪  Bayes model.
    """
    nb_estimator = GaussianNB()
    # RFE uses the given estimator to recursively eliminate features
    rfe_selector = RFE(estimator=nb_estimator,
    ↪  n_features_to_select=n_features, step=1)

    # Fit RFE on the training data
    rfe_selector.fit(X_train, y_train)

    # Transform the training and test data based on selected
    ↪  features
    X_train_rfe = rfe_selector.transform(X_train)
    X_test_rfe = rfe_selector.transform(X_test)

    # Re-train NB on the reduced set of features
    nb_estimator.fit(X_train_rfe, y_train)
    y_pred = nb_estimator.predict(X_test_rfe)

    return accuracy_score(y_test, y_pred), rfe_selector.support_

def main():
    set_seed(42)

    # Generate a synthetic classification dataset
    # 1000 samples, 20 total features, 5 informative, 2 redundant,
    ↪  random_state=42
    X, y = make_classification(n_samples=1000, n_features=20,
    ↪  n_informative=5,
                               n_redundant=2, random_state=42)

    # Split dataset into train and test
    X_train, X_test, y_train, y_test = train_test_split(X, y,
    ↪  test_size=0.3,
                                                        stratify=y,
                                                        ↪  random_state=42)

    # Demonstrate Univariate Selection (f_classif)
    uni_accuracy = demonstrate_univariate_selection(X_train, X_test,
    ↪  y_train, y_test, k=10)
    print(f"Univariate Selection (f_classif) Test Accuracy:
    ↪  {uni_accuracy:.4f}")

    # Demonstrate Mutual Information Feature Selection
    mi_accuracy = demonstrate_mutual_information(X_train, X_test,
    ↪  y_train, y_test, k=10)
    print(f"Mutual Information Selection Test Accuracy:
    ↪  {mi_accuracy:.4f}")

    # Demonstrate Recursive Feature Elimination
    rfe_accuracy, support_mask = demonstrate_rfe(X_train, X_test,
    ↪  y_train, y_test, n_features=10)
```

104

```
    print(f"RFE Selection Test Accuracy: {rfe_accuracy:.4f}")

    # Print which features RFE kept
    selected_features = np.where(support_mask == True)[0]
    print(f"RFE Selected Features: {selected_features}")

if __name__ == '__main__':
    main()
```

Key Implementation Details:

- **Dataset Generation:** A synthetic dataset is created via `make_classification` with 20 total features (some informative, some redundant) to demonstrate the effect of feature selection.

- **Univariate Feature Selection:** `SelectKBest` (with `f_classif`) filters out less-discriminative features based on ANOVA F-values. We retain the top 10, then train a Naive Bayes model.

- **Mutual Information Selection:** `SelectKBest` with `mutual_info_classif` ranks features based on mutual information with the target. The top 10 are kept for Naive Bayes training.

- **Recursive Feature Elimination (RFE):** RFE recursively removes the least-important features (based on a Naive Bayes estimator) and stops when only the desired count remains.

- **Naive Bayes Classifier:** `GaussianNB` is used as the base learner for demonstrating how feature selection can improve classification accuracy on continuous data.

Chapter 22

Handling Imbalanced Datasets with Weighted Naive Bayes

Real-world datasets often have highly skewed class distributions—for instance, rare fraud detection cases. This chapter covers strategies to improve Naive Bayes performance on minority classes, including class weighting and oversampling. You will explore how to assign customized class weights in scikit-learn, or to apply data-level techniques such as SMOTE for synthetic minority sampling. Python examples will outline data preprocessing steps, parameter adjustments, and performance comparisons to standard NB training to demonstrate how to better identify minority classes.

- Generate a synthetic dataset with a highly imbalanced class distribution.

- Train a baseline Naive Bayes model to illustrate suboptimal performance on the minority class.

- Apply class weighting via a custom sample weight array passed to `fit`.

- Use SMOTE from `imblearn` to oversample the minority class.

- Compare performance metrics (precision, recall, and f1-score) across these approaches.

Python Code Snippet

```python
import numpy as np
from sklearn.datasets import make_classification
from sklearn.model_selection import train_test_split
from sklearn.naive_bayes import GaussianNB
from sklearn.metrics import classification_report, confusion_matrix
from imblearn.over_sampling import SMOTE

def evaluate_model(model, X_test, y_test, label="Model"):
    """
    Prints classification metrics for the given model on the test
    ↪   set.
    """
    y_pred = model.predict(X_test)
    print(f"==== {label} Evaluation ====")
    print("Confusion Matrix:")
    print(confusion_matrix(y_test, y_pred))
    print("Classification Report:")
    print(classification_report(y_test, y_pred, digits=4))
    print("================================\n")

def main():
    # --------------------------------------------------------
    # 1) Create a synthetic imbalanced dataset
    # --------------------------------------------------------
    X, y = make_classification(n_samples=3000,
                               n_features=10,
                               n_informative=2,
                               n_redundant=0,
                               n_repeated=0,
                               n_clusters_per_class=1,
                               weights=[0.90, 0.10],  # 90% class 0,
                               ↪   10% class 1
                               random_state=42)

    # Split into train and test sets
    X_train, X_test, y_train, y_test = train_test_split(
        X, y, test_size=0.3, random_state=42, stratify=y
    )

    # --------------------------------------------------------
    # 2) Train a baseline Naive Bayes model
    # --------------------------------------------------------
    nb_baseline = GaussianNB()
    nb_baseline.fit(X_train, y_train)
    evaluate_model(nb_baseline, X_test, y_test, label="Baseline
    ↪   Naive Bayes")

    # --------------------------------------------------------
    # 3) Weighted Naive Bayes using sample_weight
    # --------------------------------------------------------
```

```python
    # Calculate sample weights inversely proportional to class
    ↪ frequency
    unique_classes, class_counts = np.unique(y_train,
    ↪ return_counts=True)
    total_samples = len(y_train)
    sample_weights = np.ones(total_samples, dtype=np.float64)

    for c, count in zip(unique_classes, class_counts):
        # Increase weight for minority class
        # e.g., balanced weighting = total_samples /
        ↪ (number_of_classes * count)
        sample_weights[y_train == c] = total_samples /
        ↪ (len(unique_classes) * count)

    nb_weighted = GaussianNB()
    nb_weighted.fit(X_train, y_train, sample_weight=sample_weights)
    evaluate_model(nb_weighted, X_test, y_test, label="Weighted
    ↪ Naive Bayes")

    # ----------------------------------------------------------
    # 4) Oversampling minority class with SMOTE
    # ----------------------------------------------------------
    sm = SMOTE(random_state=42)
    X_train_sm, y_train_sm = sm.fit_resample(X_train, y_train)

    nb_smote = GaussianNB()
    nb_smote.fit(X_train_sm, y_train_sm)
    evaluate_model(nb_smote, X_test, y_test, label="SMOTE + Naive
    ↪ Bayes")

    print("Imbalanced data handling complete.")

if __name__ == "__main__":
    main()
```

Key Implementation Details:

- **Baseline Model:** We train a standard Naive Bayes classifier using `fit` on the original imbalanced dataset to highlight the drawbacks of ignoring minority classes.

- **Weighted Naive Bayes:** By assigning higher `sample_weight` values to minority samples, we effectively signal the Naive Bayes algorithm to pay more attention to these examples, helping mitigate class imbalance.

- **SMOTE Oversampling:** We use `SMOTE` to synthetically generate new minority samples. This approach expands the minority class in feature space, which can improve classifier performance when data is originally scarce.

- **Evaluation Metrics:** We display the `confusion_matrix` and `classification_report` for each model to show how well the minority class is predicted under each strategy.

- **Workflow:** The `main` function integrates all steps—data splitting, baseline training, weighted training, SMOTE over-sampling, and final performance comparison.

Chapter 23

Online (Streaming) Naive Bayes with Partial Fit

Naive Bayes can be adapted to streaming scenarios where data arrives continuously. Through incremental updates, we avoid retraining from scratch for each new batch of data. This chapter provides a practical setup using scikit-learn's `partial_fit` for Mini-Batch or online learning, focusing on:

- Organizing incoming data in small batches or even single samples.

- Using a `HashingVectorizer` to map text data without retaining an ever-growing vocabulary.

- Updating the Naive Bayes model incrementally via `partial_fit`.

- Monitoring performance metrics and resource usage over time.

Python Code Snippet

```
import os
import psutil
import numpy as np
from sklearn.datasets import fetch_20newsgroups
from sklearn.feature_extraction.text import HashingVectorizer
from sklearn.naive_bayes import MultinomialNB
```

```python
from sklearn.metrics import accuracy_score

# ------------------------------------------------------------
# 1) Data streaming utility
# ------------------------------------------------------------
def stream_minibatches(data, labels, batch_size=100):
    """
    This generator yields successive batch_size chunks from the
    given data and labels. Ideal for simulating streaming data.
    """
    num_samples = len(data)
    for start_idx in range(0, num_samples, batch_size):
        end_idx = min(start_idx + batch_size, num_samples)
        yield data[start_idx:end_idx], labels[start_idx:end_idx]

# ------------------------------------------------------------
# 2) Main function: partial fit Naive Bayes on streaming data
# ------------------------------------------------------------
def main():
    # ------------------------------------------------------------
    # a) Fetch the 20 Newsgroups dataset
    # ------------------------------------------------------------
    categories = ['rec.motorcycles', 'sci.space',
    ↪   'talk.politics.guns']
    train_data = fetch_20newsgroups(subset='train',
    ↪   categories=categories, shuffle=True, random_state=42)
    test_data = fetch_20newsgroups(subset='test',
    ↪   categories=categories, shuffle=True, random_state=42)

    # ------------------------------------------------------------
    # b) Create a HashingVectorizer for streaming text
    # ------------------------------------------------------------
    # HashingVectorizer doesn't store a vocabulary dictionary,
    # which makes it suitable for incremental or streaming
    ↪   scenarios.
    vectorizer = HashingVectorizer(n_features=2**15,
    ↪   alternate_sign=False)

    # ------------------------------------------------------------
    # c) Initialize the Naive Bayes classifier
    # ------------------------------------------------------------
    # We must inform partial_fit of all possible classes upfront.
    all_classes = np.unique(train_data.target)
    nb_clf = MultinomialNB()

    # ------------------------------------------------------------
    # d) Convert the test data to features now (static for
    ↪   evaluation)
    # ------------------------------------------------------------
    X_test = vectorizer.transform(test_data.data)
    y_test = test_data.target

    # ------------------------------------------------------------
```

```python
    # e) Simulate streaming of training data in small batches
    # ------------------------------------------------------
    batch_size = 100
    epochs = 2  # Repeat streaming multiple times to simulate
    ↪   continuous flow

    print("Starting online training with partial_fit...\n")
    for epoch in range(epochs):
        print(f"=== Epoch {epoch+1}/{epochs} ===")
        # Shuffle indices for each epoch to randomize batch ordering
        indices = np.arange(len(train_data.data))
        np.random.shuffle(indices)
        data_shuffled = [train_data.data[i] for i in indices]
        labels_shuffled = train_data.target[indices]

        for i, (batch_texts, batch_labels) in
        ↪   enumerate(stream_minibatches(data_shuffled,
        ↪   labels_shuffled, batch_size)):
            # Vectorize the incoming text batch
            X_batch = vectorizer.transform(batch_texts)
            y_batch = batch_labels

            # Monitor memory usage just before partial_fit
            process = psutil.Process(os.getpid())
            mem_before = process.memory_info().rss / (1024 * 1024)

            # Incrementally train (partial_fit) with the new batch
            nb_clf.partial_fit(X_batch, y_batch,
            ↪   classes=all_classes)

            # Check memory usage after partial_fit
            mem_after = process.memory_info().rss / (1024 * 1024)

            # Periodically evaluate on the test set
            if (i + 1) % 10 == 0:
                y_pred = nb_clf.predict(X_test)
                acc = accuracy_score(y_test, y_pred)
                print(f"  Batch {i+1:03d}: Mem used:
                ↪   {mem_before:.2f}MB -> {mem_after:.2f}MB | Test
                ↪   Acc: {acc:.4f}")

    print("\nOnline training complete. Final evaluation on test
    ↪   set:")
    final_preds = nb_clf.predict(X_test)
    final_acc = accuracy_score(y_test, final_preds)
    print(f"Final Test Accuracy: {final_acc:.4f}")

if __name__ == "__main__":
    main()
```

Key Implementation Details:

- **Hashing for Incremental Vectorization:** We use `HashingVectorizer` instead of `CountVectorizer` to avoid storing vocabulary mappings. This is crucial for streaming data since new terms may appear at any time.

- **Partial Training:** The `partial_fit` method of `MultinomialNB` updates model parameters incrementally based on each batch. We supply the full class list once, ensuring the classifier is aware of all possible targets.

- **Memory Usage:** We monitor memory usage before and after each `partial_fit` call to track how the model scales with incoming data. This is helpful for production systems that require tight resource constraints.

- **Batch Size and Epochs:** Streaming can be done in near real-time (batch size = 1), or in larger blocks. We illustrate mini-batching with a `batch_size` of 100 for efficiency.

- **Metric Tracking:** By periodically evaluating on a hold-out test set, we can observe performance drift and decide when to adjust hyperparameters or data collection strategies in a real production environment.

Chapter 24

Hierarchical Classification for Product Categorization

Complex product catalogs, such as e-commerce platforms, often involve hierarchical taxonomies (e.g., Electronics > Computers > Laptops). This chapter describes an approach that uses Naive Bayes classifiers at each node of the hierarchy, refining product labels step by step. You will see how to break down the classification challenge into multiple sub-classifications within each branch. Will detail building multiple NB models for each level, processing product text or attribute data, and cascading predictions down the hierarchy.

Python Code Snippet

```python
import pandas as pd
import numpy as np
from sklearn.model_selection import train_test_split
from sklearn.feature_extraction.text import TfidfVectorizer
from sklearn.naive_bayes import MultinomialNB
from sklearn.pipeline import Pipeline
from sklearn.metrics import accuracy_score

# ------------------------------------------------------------
# 1) Sample Hierarchical E-commerce Data
# ------------------------------------------------------------
```

```python
# In practice, you would load this from a file or database.
# For demonstration, we simulate a small dataset with two levels:
#    Top-level: Electronics or Clothing
#    Sub-level for Electronics: Computers or MobilePhones
#    Sub-level for Clothing: Shirts or Shoes

data = [
    # Electronics -> Computers
    {"product_id": 1, "text": "Laptop with 16GB RAM for
    ↪   professionals", "top_category": "Electronics",
    ↪   "sub_category": "Computers"},
    {"product_id": 2, "text": "Desktop computer with powerful
    ↪   graphics card", "top_category": "Electronics",
    ↪   "sub_category": "Computers"},
    {"product_id": 3, "text": "Gaming laptop with the latest
    ↪   processor", "top_category": "Electronics", "sub_category":
    ↪   "Computers"},

    # Electronics -> MobilePhones
    {"product_id": 4, "text": "Smartphone with high resolution
    ↪   camera", "top_category": "Electronics", "sub_category":
    ↪   "MobilePhones"},
    {"product_id": 5, "text": "Mobile phone featuring large display
    ↪   and fast charging", "top_category": "Electronics",
    ↪   "sub_category": "MobilePhones"},

    # Clothing -> Shirts
    {"product_id": 6, "text": "Men's cotton T-Shirt with printed
    ↪   design", "top_category": "Clothing", "sub_category":
    ↪   "Shirts"},
    {"product_id": 7, "text": "Formal shirt for office wear",
    ↪   "top_category": "Clothing", "sub_category": "Shirts"},
    {"product_id": 8, "text": "Casual summer shirt in bright
    ↪   colors", "top_category": "Clothing", "sub_category":
    ↪   "Shirts"},

    # Clothing -> Shoes
    {"product_id": 9, "text": "Running shoes with breathable mesh",
    ↪   "top_category": "Clothing", "sub_category": "Shoes"},
    {"product_id": 10, "text": "Leather shoes suitable for formal
    ↪   events", "top_category": "Clothing", "sub_category":
    ↪   "Shoes"}
]

df = pd.DataFrame(data)

# ------------------------------------------------------------
# 2) Split the Dataset for Top-Level Classification
# ------------------------------------------------------------
# We'll hold out some data for testing the top-level classifier.
X_top = df["text"]
y_top = df["top_category"]
```

```python
X_train_top, X_test_top, y_train_top, y_test_top =
↪   train_test_split(X_top, y_top, test_size=0.3, random_state=42,
↪   stratify=y_top)

# ------------------------------------------------------------
# 3) Build a Naive Bayes Pipeline for Top-Level Classification
# ------------------------------------------------------------
top_level_pipeline = Pipeline([
    ("tfidf", TfidfVectorizer()),
    ("nb", MultinomialNB())
])

top_level_pipeline.fit(X_train_top, y_train_top)

# Evaluate on top-level test set
y_pred_top = top_level_pipeline.predict(X_test_top)
accuracy_top = accuracy_score(y_test_top, y_pred_top)
print("Top-Level Classification Accuracy:", accuracy_top)

# ------------------------------------------------------------
# 4) Train Separate Sub-Classifiers for Each Top-Level Category
# ------------------------------------------------------------
# We'll group the data by top_category and train a sub-classifier
↪   for each group.
sub_pipelines = {}

unique_top_categories = df["top_category"].unique()
for cat in unique_top_categories:
    # Extract subset of data for this top-category
    subset = df[df["top_category"] == cat]
    X_sub = subset["text"]
    y_sub = subset["sub_category"]

    # Train/test split for sub-level classification
    X_train_sub, X_test_sub, y_train_sub, y_test_sub =
    ↪   train_test_split(
        X_sub, y_sub, test_size=0.3, random_state=42, stratify=y_sub
    )

    # Build sub-level pipeline
    pipeline_sub = Pipeline([
        ("tfidf", TfidfVectorizer()),
        ("nb", MultinomialNB())
    ])
    pipeline_sub.fit(X_train_sub, y_train_sub)

    # Evaluate sub-level classifier for this category
    y_pred_sub = pipeline_sub.predict(X_test_sub)
    accuracy_sub = accuracy_score(y_test_sub, y_pred_sub)
    print(f"Sub-Level Classification Accuracy for {cat}:",
    ↪   accuracy_sub)

    # Store the trained pipeline
```

```
    sub_pipelines[cat] = pipeline_sub

# --------------------------------------------------------------
# 5) Hierarchical Prediction Mechanism
# --------------------------------------------------------------
def predict_hierarchy(product_text):
    """
    Predict the top-level category using the top-level classifier,
    then pass the text to the corresponding sub-level classifier.
    """
    predicted_top = top_level_pipeline.predict([product_text])[0]
    predicted_sub =
    ↪   sub_pipelines[predicted_top].predict([product_text])[0]
    return predicted_top, predicted_sub

# --------------------------------------------------------------
# 6) Demo on Test Samples
# --------------------------------------------------------------
# We will combine the top-level test set with sub-level predictions
# and see how we do in a hierarchical manner.
test_samples = X_test_top.tolist()
true_top_labels = y_test_top.tolist()

# We'll attempt to retrieve sub-level labels from the original df
↪   for a direct check
# if we can find them in the test set. For a real scenario, you'd
↪   keep a separate sub-level test set.
correct_hierarchical_predictions = 0
total_checked = 0

for idx, text_sample in enumerate(test_samples):
    # True top-level
    true_top = true_top_labels[idx]

    # In a real system, you'd have the ground-truth sub-level label
    ↪   stored or known:
    # For demonstration, let's try to match the data in df
    matched_row = df[df["text"] == text_sample]
    if len(matched_row) == 1:
        true_sub = matched_row.iloc[0]["sub_category"]
        pred_top, pred_sub = predict_hierarchy(text_sample)
        print(f"\nText: {text_sample}")
        print(f"True Hierarchy: ({true_top}, {true_sub})")
        print(f"Predicted Hierarchy: ({pred_top}, {pred_sub})")

        if (pred_top == true_top) and (pred_sub == true_sub):
            correct_hierarchical_predictions += 1
        total_checked += 1

if total_checked > 0:
    overall_accuracy = correct_hierarchical_predictions /
    ↪   total_checked
```

```
    print(f"\nOverall Hierarchical Accuracy on Available Samples:
    ↪   {overall_accuracy:.2f}")
else:
    print("\nNo overlapping test samples found for sub-level
    ↪   checking.")

# --------------------------------------------------------------
# 7) Inference on New Unseen Products
# --------------------------------------------------------------
new_products = [
    "A brand new smartphone with fast processor",
    "Stylish running shoes for marathon runners",
    "Desktop PC optimized for gaming performance",
    "Formal cotton shirt for office"
]

for prod_text in new_products:
    top_cat, sub_cat = predict_hierarchy(prod_text)
    print(f"\nNew Product Description: {prod_text}")
    print(f"Predicted Hierarchy: {top_cat} > {sub_cat}")
```

Key Implementation Details:

- **Top-Level Classifier:** We train a single Naive Bayes classifier (`MultinomialNB`) on the top-level categories (e.g., Electronics vs. Clothing). This classifier uses text features extracted via `TfidfVectorizer`.

- **Per-Node Sub-Classifiers:** For each top-level category, we train another Naive Bayes classifier on the subset of products belonging to that category. This approach cleanly modularizes each sub-level model.

- **Hierarchical Prediction**: First, we predict the parent (top) category, then route the product text to the appropriate sub-category pipeline. This cascaded prediction structure refines labels step by step in a tree-like manner.

- **Data Splitting**: Each node's classifier (top-level or sub-level) is trained and evaluated with its own train-test split. This ensures that performance comparisons remain consistent across levels.

- **Scikit-learn Pipelines**: Using `Pipeline` helps combine feature extraction (TF-IDF) with the Naive Bayes estimator, making the model self-contained and easier to reuse for inference.

118

- **Example Usage**: We tested hierarchical accuracy on held-out samples and demonstrated classification of new products into appropriate categories. In a production setting, you would scale up this approach to more levels and incorporate dataset-specific tuning.

Chapter 25

Time-series Classification with Naive Bayes

Naive Bayes can also be leveraged for certain forms of time-series classification. You will learn how to transform segments of signal or temporal data into feature vectors (mean, standard deviation, frequency components). Then, a Gaussian Naive Bayes or MultinomialNB (if features are quantized) can be trained to label each segment. Python implementations will show how to process time-series data, generate overlapping windows, and build a classifier that distinguishes events (e.g., machine states, physiological signals) over time.

- First, we collect or generate time-series data, ensuring each sample (or continuous recording) has an associated label.

- Next, we divide or slide through each time-series with overlapping windows, isolating shorter segments of the signal.

- We compute representative features for each window (e.g., mean, standard deviation, or power in specific frequency bands).

- These window-level features are treated as samples in a supervised classification setting. A Naive Bayes classifier is fit to map feature vectors to categorical labels (event types, states, etc.).

- Finally, we can evaluate the model with standard metrics (accuracy, confusion matrix, classification report), and use it to predict labels for new, unseen time-series segments in real-world applications.

Python Code Snippet

```python
import numpy as np
import pandas as pd
from scipy.fft import rfft, rfftfreq
from sklearn.model_selection import train_test_split
from sklearn.naive_bayes import GaussianNB, MultinomialNB
from sklearn.metrics import accuracy_score, confusion_matrix,
↪   classification_report
import matplotlib.pyplot as plt

def generate_synthetic_time_series(num_samples=300, length=128,
↪   num_classes=3, noise_level=0.1):
    """
    Generate synthetic time-series data with different frequencies
    ↪   for each class.

    Returns:
        data: np.array of shape (num_samples, length)
        labels: np.array of shape (num_samples,)
    """
    # Pre-allocate arrays
    data = np.zeros((num_samples, length))
    labels = np.zeros(num_samples, dtype=int)

    # Frequencies associated with each class
    class_freqs = np.linspace(5, 20, num_classes)   # e.g., 5 Hz,
    ↪   12.5 Hz, 20 Hz for 3 classes

    samples_per_class = num_samples // num_classes
    t = np.linspace(0, 1, length, endpoint=False)

    idx = 0
    for cl in range(num_classes):
        freq = class_freqs[cl]
        for _ in range(samples_per_class):
            # Generate a sine wave
            sine_wave = np.sin(2 * np.pi * freq * t)
            # Add random noise
            noisy_wave = sine_wave + noise_level *
            ↪   np.random.randn(len(t))
            data[idx, :] = noisy_wave
            labels[idx] = cl
            idx += 1
```

```python
    # If num_samples is not perfectly divisible by num_classes, fill
    ↪   the remainder
    while idx < num_samples:
        cl = np.random.randint(0, num_classes)
        freq = class_freqs[cl]
        sine_wave = np.sin(2 * np.pi * freq * t)
        noisy_wave = sine_wave + noise_level *
        ↪   np.random.randn(len(t))
        data[idx, :] = noisy_wave
        labels[idx] = cl
        idx += 1

    # Shuffle the dataset to avoid ordering effects
    shuffle_indices = np.random.permutation(num_samples)
    data = data[shuffle_indices]
    labels = labels[shuffle_indices]

    return data, labels

def create_overlapping_windows(data, labels, window_size=32,
↪   overlap=16):
    """
    Convert an array of time-series samples into overlapping
    ↪   windows.

    Args:
        data: np.array of shape (num_samples, time_length)
        labels: np.array of shape (num_samples,)
        window_size: int, size of each window
        overlap: int, length of overlap between consecutive windows

    Returns:
        windowed_data: list of np.array, each array of shape
        ↪   (window_size,)
        windowed_labels: list of int, label assigned to that window
    """
    windowed_data = []
    windowed_labels = []

    for i in range(len(data)):
        series = data[i]
        label = labels[i]
        start = 0
        end = window_size

        # Slide over each sample with overlap
        while end <= len(series):
            segment = series[start:end]
            windowed_data.append(segment)
            windowed_labels.append(label)
            start += (window_size - overlap)
            end = start + window_size
```

```python
    # Convert to np.array for easier handling and shaping
    windowed_data = np.array(windowed_data)
    windowed_labels = np.array(windowed_labels, dtype=int)
    return windowed_data, windowed_labels

def extract_features(windows):
    """
    Extract features from each window: mean, std, and dominant
    ↪  frequency.
    Args:
        windows: np.array of shape (num_windows, window_size)
    Returns:
        features: np.array of shape (num_windows, 3) [mean, std,
        ↪  dominant_frequency]
    """
    num_windows = windows.shape[0]
    features = np.zeros((num_windows, 3))

    for i, win in enumerate(windows):
        # 1) Mean
        mean_val = np.mean(win)

        # 2) Std
        std_val = np.std(win)

        # 3) Dominant frequency (magnitude)
        # Apply real FFT to the window
        fft_vals = np.abs(rfft(win))
        # Exclude the 0-frequency term for "dominant" frequency if
        ↪  desired:
        dominant_freq = np.argmax(fft_vals[1:]) + 1  # +1 to offset
        ↪  the slice

        features[i] = [mean_val, std_val, dominant_freq]

    return features

def main():
    # 1) Generate synthetic time-series data
    data, labels = generate_synthetic_time_series(
        num_samples=300, length=128, num_classes=3, noise_level=0.2
    )

    # 2) Create overlapping windows
    windows, window_labels = create_overlapping_windows(
        data, labels, window_size=32, overlap=16
    )

    # 3) Extract features from each window
    X = extract_features(windows)
    y = window_labels
```

```python
    # For demonstration, we can either use GaussianNB or
    ↪   MultinomialNB
    # If features were quantized or purely integer counts,
    ↪   Multinomial might be more appropriate.
    # We'll use GaussianNB here:
    classifier = GaussianNB()

    # 4) Train/test split
    X_train, X_test, y_train, y_test = train_test_split(
        X, y, test_size=0.3, random_state=42, stratify=y
    )

    # 5) Fit the classifier
    classifier.fit(X_train, y_train)

    # 6) Evaluate on the test set
    y_pred = classifier.predict(X_test)

    acc = accuracy_score(y_test, y_pred)
    print(f"Accuracy on test set: {acc:.2f}")

    # 7) Print confusion matrix and classification report
    cm = confusion_matrix(y_test, y_pred)
    print("Confusion Matrix:")
    print(cm)

    report = classification_report(y_test, y_pred)
    print("Classification Report:")
    print(report)

    # (Optional) Quick plot of a random series vs. predicted label
    idx = np.random.randint(0, len(X_test))
    sample_features = X_test[idx:idx+1]
    true_label = y_test[idx]
    pred_label = classifier.predict(sample_features)[0]

    print(f"Random Sample True Label: {true_label}, Predicted:
    ↪   {pred_label}")

    # Just to give an example of the raw time-series that formed the
    ↪   window
    # This is not strictly necessary, but helps illustrate the data.
    plt.figure(figsize=(8, 3))
    plt.plot(windows[idx], label="Window Data")
    plt.title(f"Time-series Window (Label: {true_label}, Predicted:
    ↪   {pred_label})")
    plt.legend()
    plt.show()

if __name__ == "__main__":
    main()
```

Key Implementation Details:

- **Data Generation:** We call `generate_synthetic_time_series` to create a simple labeled dataset, where each class has a distinct sine wave frequency with added noise. This provides a controlled environment to test segmentation and classification.

- **Overlapping Windows:** The function `create_overlapping_windows` forms segmented windows of a fixed size with a specified overlap. Each window inherits the label of the longer time-series from which it originated.

- **Feature Extraction:** `extract_features` computes the mean, standard deviation, and dominant frequency within each window. These features capture both time-domain and (simplistic) frequency-domain characteristics.

- **Naive Bayes Classifier:** We employ `GaussianNB` to handle continuous-valued features. If the data were strictly integer counts or quantized, `MultinomialNB` might be more appropriate.

- **Evaluation:** After training, we use `accuracy_score`, `confusion_matrix`, and `classification_report` to measure model performance on a held-out test set.

- **Example Inspection:** The example code also shows a randomly selected window from the test set, plotting the raw time-series segment and comparing true vs. predicted labels, illustrating how segments relate to classification outcomes.

Chapter 26

Cross-lingual Text Classification Using Naive Bayes

In cross-lingual classification, trained models can be applied to text in multiple languages with minimal re-training. You will learn techniques such as word translation or bilingual dictionaries to unify feature spaces across languages. This chapter's Python implementations demonstrate how to train an NB model on a primary language dataset, align feature vocabularies, and classify documents in other languages. Key steps include:

- normalizing text,

- selectively translating or ignoring certain tokens,

- optimizing the pipeline for multi-language usage.

Python Code Snippet

```python
import re
import random
import numpy as np
import pandas as pd
from sklearn.model_selection import train_test_split
from sklearn.feature_extraction.text import TfidfVectorizer
from sklearn.naive_bayes import MultinomialNB
from sklearn.metrics import accuracy_score, classification_report
```

```python
# ------------------------------------------------------------
# 1) Synthetic bilingual data and dictionary
# ------------------------------------------------------------
# For a real scenario, you would load or scrape data in different
#   languages.
# Here, we create two small labeled datasets: one in English, one in
#   Spanish.
# Suppose these items are about "tech" or "sports" as example
#   categories.

english_texts = [
    "Latest smartphone releases have amazing features",
    "The football match was thrilling last night",
    "Software updates can improve performance over time",
    "Tennis championships are widely watched globally"
]
english_labels = ["tech", "sports", "tech", "sports"]

spanish_texts = [
    "El lanzamiento de teléfonos inteligentes tiene características
       asombrosas",
    "El partido de fútbol fue emocionante anoche",
    "Las actualizaciones de software pueden mejorar el rendimiento
       con el tiempo",
    "Los torneos de tenis se ven en todo el mundo"
]
spanish_labels = ["tech", "sports", "tech", "sports"]

# A simple bilingual dictionary from English to Spanish tokens.
# In practice, more robust dictionaries or translation APIs would be
#   used.
bilingual_dict = {
    "latest": "ultimo",
    "smartphone": "teléfono inteligente",
    "releases": "lanzamientos",
    "features": "características",
    "football": "fútbol",
    "match": "partido",
    "thrilling": "emocionante",
    "software": "software",    # same
    "updates": "actualizaciones",
    "improve": "mejorar",
    "performance": "rendimiento",
    "time": "tiempo",
    "tennis": "tenis",
    "championships": "torneos",
    "are": "son",
    "widely": "ampliamente",
    "watched": "visto"
}

# ------------------------------------------------------------
```

```
# 2) Token translation / normalizing utilities
# ------------------------------------------------------------
def simple_preprocess(text):
    """
    A simple text preprocessing that lowercases, removes
    ↪ punctuation,
    and splits on whitespace.
    """
    text = text.lower()
    text = re.sub(r"[^a-záéíóúñü]+", " ", text)
    return text.strip().split()

def align_tokens_to_spanish(tokens, bilingual_map):
    """
    For each English token, check if it exists in bilingual_map.
    If yes, translate. If no, keep the token as is (or optionally
    ↪ discard).
    This would unify tokens under Spanish for cross-lingual usage.
    """
    aligned = []
    for tk in tokens:
        if tk in bilingual_map:
            # Replace English token with Spanish equivalent
            aligned.append(bilingual_map[tk])
        else:
            # If token is already Spanish or we don't have a
            ↪ mapping, keep it
            aligned.append(tk)
    return aligned

def unify_text(text, bilingual_map):
    """
    Unifies text to Spanish tokens where possible, returning a
    ↪ string
    that can be used by a vectorizer.
    """
    tokens = simple_preprocess(text)
    aligned_tokens = align_tokens_to_spanish(tokens, bilingual_map)
    return " ".join(aligned_tokens)

# ------------------------------------------------------------
# 3) Combine data and unify to a single language representation
# ------------------------------------------------------------

# Combine English and Spanish datasets
all_texts = english_texts + spanish_texts
all_labels = english_labels + spanish_labels

# Translate/normalize them into Spanish representation (where
↪ possible)
unified_texts = [unify_text(txt, bilingual_dict) for txt in
↪ all_texts]
```

```python
# -------------------------------------------------------------
# 4) Train-test split
# -------------------------------------------------------------
train_texts, test_texts, train_labels, test_labels =
↪    train_test_split(
    unified_texts, all_labels, test_size=0.3, random_state=42
)


# -------------------------------------------------------------
# 5) Vectorize text and build a NB pipeline
# -------------------------------------------------------------
# The core emphasis is on the Naive Bayes portion.
# We use TfidfVectorizer to convert text into feature vectors, then
↪    MultinomialNB to classify.

tfidf_vectorizer = TfidfVectorizer()
X_train = tfidf_vectorizer.fit_transform(train_texts)
X_test = tfidf_vectorizer.transform(test_texts)

# Instantiate the Naive Bayes classifier
nb_classifier = MultinomialNB()

# Train
nb_classifier.fit(X_train, train_labels)

# -------------------------------------------------------------
# 6) Evaluate model performance
# -------------------------------------------------------------
predictions = nb_classifier.predict(X_test)
accuracy = accuracy_score(test_labels, predictions)
print("Accuracy on test set: {:.2f}%".format(accuracy * 100))
print("Classification Report:\n", classification_report(test_labels,
↪    predictions))

# -------------------------------------------------------------
# 7) Demonstration of classifying a new text in English or Spanish
# -------------------------------------------------------------
def classify_new_text(new_text, bilingual_map, vectorizer, model):
    """
    Given a new text, unify it to Spanish tokens, vectorize, predict
    ↪    with NB model.
    """
    unified_str = unify_text(new_text, bilingual_map)
    vec = vectorizer.transform([unified_str])
    pred_label = model.predict(vec)[0]
    return pred_label

# Example usage
test_sentence_eng = "The new smartphone has powerful software
↪    features"
test_sentence_spa = "Los últimos lanzamientos de teléfonos
↪    inteligentes"
```

129

```
print("English text prediction:",
↪  classify_new_text(test_sentence_eng, bilingual_dict,
↪  tfidf_vectorizer, nb_classifier))
print("Spanish text prediction:",
↪  classify_new_text(test_sentence_spa, bilingual_dict,
↪  tfidf_vectorizer, nb_classifier))
```

Key Implementation Details:

- **Data Preparation:** We created small synthetic examples in English and Spanish, each labeled for classification (e.g., "tech" vs. "sports"). In practice, you would collect real-world text data in multiple languages.

- **Bilingual Dictionary:** A minimal `bilingual_dict` is used to map English tokens to Spanish. Unknown or already Spanish tokens remain the same, unifying vocabulary.

- **Text Normalization:** The function `simple_preprocess` lowercases text and strips punctuation. The function `align_tokens_to_spanish` replaces tokens based on `bilingual_dict`.

- **Naive Bayes Classifier:** `MultinomialNB` learns label distributions over features generated by `TfidfVectorizer`. This approach effectively handles text data frequency distributions.

- **Cross-lingual Unification:** By mapping English tokens into Spanish space, the classifier can treat all tokens as part of the same feature set.

- **Extended Usage:** You can leverage larger translation dictionaries or advanced translation APIs for real-world scenarios, integrate domain-specific expansions, and experiment with `BernoulliNB` or `GaussianNB` if data characteristics differ.

Chapter 27

SMOTE and Naive Bayes for Minority Class Detection

Continuing the conversation on imbalanced data, this chapter shows the combination of SMOTE (Synthetic Minority Over-sampling Technique) with Naive Bayes, which can significantly enhance minority class detection. You will review how SMOTE synthetic samples are generated, then apply them to training data before feeding into NB. Will illustrate the process: splitting data, oversampling the minority class, and training the classifier. The chapter highlights possible pitfalls of oversampling and how to tune SMOTE parameters effectively.

- First, we create an imbalanced dataset with a significant minority class shortage.

- Next, we split this dataset into training and test sets.

- We apply `SMOTE` on the training split to oversample the minority class by synthesizing new, plausible minority samples.

- We then train a Naive Bayes classifier on the augmented training data and evaluate it on the untouched test set.

- Finally, we discuss class distribution shifts and potential pitfalls of oversampling, such as overfitting or generating noisy points.

Python Code Snippet

```python
import numpy as np
import pandas as pd
import random

from sklearn.datasets import make_classification
from sklearn.model_selection import train_test_split
from sklearn.naive_bayes import GaussianNB
from sklearn.metrics import classification_report, confusion_matrix
from imblearn.over_sampling import SMOTE

#
↪   ------------------------------------------------------------------
# 1) Utility Function to Set Random Seeds for Reproducibility
#
↪   ------------------------------------------------------------------
def set_seed(seed=42):
    random.seed(seed)
    np.random.seed(seed)


#
↪   ------------------------------------------------------------------
# 2) Generate Synthetic Imbalanced Dataset
#
↪   ------------------------------------------------------------------
def generate_data(n_samples=1000):
    """
    Generates a synthetic binary classification dataset
    with a large imbalance between majority and minority classes.
    """
    X, y = make_classification(
        n_samples=n_samples,
        n_features=5,          # number of features
        n_informative=3,       # number of informative features
        n_redundant=0,
        n_clusters_per_class=2,
        weights=[0.9, 0.1],    # 90% majority, 10% minority
        random_state=42
    )
    return X, y


#
↪   ------------------------------------------------------------------
# 3) Train Naive Bayes Classifier After Applying SMOTE
#
↪   ------------------------------------------------------------------
def train_naive_bayes_with_smote(X_train, y_train, X_test, y_test):
    """
    Applies SMOTE to the training set and fits a Gaussian Naive
    ↪   Bayes model.
    Returns the trained model and prints evaluation metrics.
```

```python
    """
    # SMOTE oversampling
    smote = SMOTE(random_state=42)
    X_train_res, y_train_res = smote.fit_resample(X_train, y_train)

    # Create and train the Naive Bayes classifier
    nb_classifier = GaussianNB()
    nb_classifier.fit(X_train_res, y_train_res)

    # Evaluate on test data
    y_pred = nb_classifier.predict(X_test)

    print("Classification Report on Test Data:")
    print(classification_report(y_test, y_pred, digits=4))

    print("Confusion Matrix on Test Data:")
    print(confusion_matrix(y_test, y_pred))

    return nb_classifier

#
↪   ------------------------------------------------------------------
# 4) Main Routine to Tie Everything Together
#
↪   ------------------------------------------------------------------
def main():
    # Set seed for reproducibility
    set_seed(42)

    # Generate data
    X, y = generate_data(n_samples=2000)

    # Split into train/test
    X_train, X_test, y_train, y_test = train_test_split(
        X, y, test_size=0.3, random_state=42, stratify=y
    )

    # Train NB with SMOTE
    model = train_naive_bayes_with_smote(X_train, y_train, X_test,
    ↪   y_test)

    # The trained model can be used further for predictions
    # For example:
    sample_data = [X_test[0]]   # Test with a single sample
    prediction = model.predict(sample_data)
    print(f"Sample Data Prediction: {prediction}")

if __name__ == "__main__":
    main()
```

Key Implementation Details:

- **Data Generation:** We use `make_classification` to construct a synthetic dataset with a predefined level of class imbalance (90

- **SMOTE Oversampling:** The `SMOTE` algorithm synthesizes new minority samples by interpolating between existing minority data points. We strictly apply it to the training set only, preventing data leakage into the test set.

- **Naive Bayes Classifier:** A `GaussianNB` classifier is used as the main learning algorithm. This variant assumes continuous-valued inputs are normally distributed; it is straightforward, fast, and effective for many numeric datasets.

- **Evaluation:** We predict on the test set (untouched by oversampling) to measure real-world performance. The `classification_report` and `confusion_matrix` help identify gains in minority class recall and potential changes in overall accuracy.

- **Potential Pitfalls:** While SMOTE can improve minority recall, it may also produce borderline samples or outliers. Tuning SMOTE parameters (`k_neighbors`, `sampling_strategy`, etc.) or using advanced oversampling variants (`BorderlineSMOTE, ADASYN`) can help mitigate noisy synthetic points.

Chapter 28

Transfer Learning with Naive Bayes

This chapter addresses using a Naive Bayes model trained on one domain to help classify data in another domain with limited labeled examples. You will practice aligning feature distributions from the source and target domains by re-weighting or re-labeling. Python examples involve adjusting priors or partially retraining the classifier with a small sample of target-domain data. The chapter details how to incorporate domain adaptation approaches so that NB remains effective despite domain shifts.

- We first train a Naive Bayes classifier on a "source domain" dataset.

- Then we present a small labeled sample from the "target domain," which has typical domain shifts (e.g., different feature distributions).

- We incorporate this new target-domain data via a partial update (or "partial fit") on the Naive Bayes model, optionally with re-weighting to emphasize newer examples.

- We measure how the adapted classifier performs on the target domain compared to the unadapted source-only model.

Python Code Snippet

```python
import numpy as np
from sklearn.naive_bayes import GaussianNB
from sklearn.metrics import accuracy_score
from sklearn.model_selection import train_test_split

def generate_synthetic_data(num_samples=500, center=0.0,
↪   random_seed=42):
    """
    Generates a 2D synthetic dataset for a binary classification
    ↪   task.
    Labels are assigned based on the sign of the sum of
    ↪   x-coordinates:
        y = 0 if (x1 + x2) < 0
        y = 1 otherwise.
    The 'center' parameter shifts the mean of the distribution,
    simulating domain differences.
    """
    np.random.seed(random_seed)
    X = np.random.randn(num_samples, 2) + center
    y = (X[:, 0] + X[:, 1] >= 0).astype(int)
    return X, y

def train_source_model(X_source, y_source):
    """
    Trains a Gaussian Naive Bayes model on source-domain data
    and returns the fitted model.
    """
    model = GaussianNB()
    model.fit(X_source, y_source)
    return model

def evaluate_model(model, X_test, y_test, domain_name=""):
    """
    Evaluates the model on given test data and prints out accuracy.
    """
    preds = model.predict(X_test)
    acc = accuracy_score(y_test, preds)
    print(f"Accuracy on {domain_name} data: {acc:.4f}")
    return acc

def adapt_model_with_target_data(model, X_target, y_target,
↪   weight=1.0):
    """
    Demonstrates partial domain adaptation by updating (partial_fit)
    the existing NB model with new target-domain data.
    Optionally applies a uniform sample_weight to emphasize or
    ↪   de-emphasize
    the new domain data.
    """
    # GaussianNB supports 'partial_fit' for incremental updates.
```

136

```python
    # The 'classes_' must include all possible class labels [0, 1].
    sample_weights = np.ones_like(y_target, dtype=float) * weight
    model.partial_fit(X_target, y_target, classes=[0, 1],
    ↪    sample_weight=sample_weights)
    return model

def main():
    # 1. Generate source-domain training data
    X_source, y_source = generate_synthetic_data(num_samples=500,
    ↪    center=0.0, random_seed=42)
    X_source_train, X_source_val, y_source_train, y_source_val =
    ↪    train_test_split(
        X_source, y_source, test_size=0.2, random_state=42
    )

    # 2. Generate target-domain data (different center -> domain
    ↪    shift)
    X_target, y_target = generate_synthetic_data(num_samples=200,
    ↪    center=2.0, random_seed=24)
    X_target_train, X_target_val, y_target_train, y_target_val =
    ↪    train_test_split(
        X_target, y_target, test_size=0.5, random_state=24
    )

    # 3. Train NB model only on source data
    nb_model_source = train_source_model(X_source_train,
    ↪    y_source_train)

    # 4. Evaluate on source validation set
    print("Before Adaptation:")
    evaluate_model(nb_model_source, X_source_val, y_source_val,
    ↪    domain_name="Source-Val")
    # 5. Evaluate on target data
    evaluate_model(nb_model_source, X_target_val, y_target_val,
    ↪    domain_name="Target-Val")

    # 6. Adapt the model by partial-fitting on a small portion of
    ↪    target data
    #    (Simulate limited labeled examples from the target domain)
    #    We'll emphasize these new samples by doubling their weight.
    nb_model_adapted = adapt_model_with_target_data(
        nb_model_source, X_target_train[:50], y_target_train[:50],
        ↪    weight=2.0
    )

    # 7. Evaluate the adapted model on target data
    print("\nAfter Adaptation:")
    evaluate_model(nb_model_adapted, X_source_val, y_source_val,
    ↪    domain_name="Source-Val")
    evaluate_model(nb_model_adapted, X_target_val, y_target_val,
    ↪    domain_name="Target-Val")

if __name__ == "__main__":
```

137

Key Implementation Details:

- **Data Generation:** We create separate source and target datasets by shifting the mean of the distributions, mimicking domain drift. Class labels are assigned based on a simple threshold, and we demonstrate how misalignment may occur when the data distribution changes.

- **Naive Bayes Classifier:** We use `GaussianNB` to handle continuous domain features. This model is first fit on source data alone.

- **Partial Fit for Domain Adaptation:** The function `adapt_model_with_target_data` illustrates how to incorporate new data from the target domain incrementally. We use `partial_fit`, which updates the model's parameters without discarding knowledge gained from the source domain.

- **Sample Weighting:** Setting a higher `weight` emphasizes the significance of newly acquired target examples, helping the classifier adapt its priors and likelihood estimates more aggressively toward the target domain distribution.

- **Evaluations:** We measure accuracy on both source-validation and target-validation splits before and after partially adapting the model. Typically, we expect improved performance on the target domain with minimal degradation on the source domain.

Chapter 29

Social Media Post Classification Using Text Embeddings and Naive Bayes

You will learn how to enhance Naive Bayes by using dense text embeddings, such as word2vec or GloVe, to represent text data. The approach involves averaging or summing embedding vectors for each document, then treating these as real-valued features in a GaussianNB model. Will walk through loading a pre-trained embedding model, converting raw posts into embedding features, training GaussianNB, and interpreting how textual meaning is captured in the classification process.

Python Code Snippet

```
import os
import re
import zipfile
import requests
import numpy as np
import pandas as pd
from io import BytesIO
from sklearn.model_selection import train_test_split
from sklearn.naive_bayes import GaussianNB
```

```python
from sklearn.metrics import classification_report, confusion_matrix
import nltk
from nltk.corpus import stopwords
nltk.download('stopwords')

# ------------------------------------------------------------
# 1) Utility to download and load GloVe embeddings
# ------------------------------------------------------------
def load_glove_embeddings(embeddings_dim=50):
    """
    Downloads a minimal GloVe embedding file if not present,
    loads it into a dictionary: {word: embedding_vector}.
    """
    glove_file = f"glove.6B.{embeddings_dim}d.txt"
    if not os.path.isfile(glove_file):
        print(f"Downloading GloVe {embeddings_dim}D embeddings. This
        ↪  may take a while...")
        url = "http://nlp.stanford.edu/data/glove.6B.zip"
        response = requests.get(url, stream=True)
        if response.status_code == 200:
            with zipfile.ZipFile(BytesIO(response.content)) as z:
                with z.open(glove_file) as f:
                    lines = f.readlines()
                with open(glove_file, "wb") as out_f:
                    for line in lines:
                        out_f.write(line)
        else:
            raise RuntimeError("Error downloading embeddings from
            ↪  the provided URL.")
    # Now load embeddings into a dictionary
    embeddings_dict = {}
    with open(glove_file, 'r', encoding="utf-8") as f:
        for line in f:
            values = line.split()
            word = values[0]
            vector = np.asarray(values[1:], dtype='float32')
            embeddings_dict[word] = vector
    return embeddings_dict


# ------------------------------------------------------------
# 2) Preprocessing function for text
# ------------------------------------------------------------
def preprocess_text(text):
    """
    Removes URLs, handles punctuation and lowercasing,
    optionally removes stopwords.
    """
    # Remove URLs
    text = re.sub(r"http\S+|www\S+|https\S+", '', text,
    ↪  flags=re.MULTILINE)
    # Remove user mentions and hashtags (common in social media)
    text = re.sub(r"@\w+|#\w+", '', text)
    # Remove non-alphanumeric characters (except spaces)
```

140

```python
    text = re.sub(r"[^a-zA-Z0-9\s]", '', text)
    # Lowercase
    text = text.lower().strip()
    # Remove stopwords (optional)
    stop_words = set(stopwords.words('english'))
    words = [w for w in text.split() if w not in stop_words]
    # Rejoin
    processed_text = " ".join(words)
    return processed_text


# -------------------------------------------------------------
# 3) Convert each text into an average embedding
# -------------------------------------------------------------
def create_embedding_features(texts, embeddings_dict,
↪    embeddings_dim=50):
    """
    Splits each text into tokens, looks up GloVe embeddings,
    and aggregates them by averaging. If a token is missing,
    it is skipped; if no tokens are matched, returns zeros.
    """
    features = []
    for text in texts:
        tokens = text.split()
        valid_embeddings = []
        for token in tokens:
            if token in embeddings_dict:
                valid_embeddings.append(embeddings_dict[token])
        if len(valid_embeddings) == 0:
            # No tokens matched, use zeros
            features.append(np.zeros(embeddings_dim,
↪            dtype='float32'))
        else:
            # Average the embeddings
            avg_vec = np.mean(valid_embeddings, axis=0)
            features.append(avg_vec)
    return np.array(features)


# -------------------------------------------------------------
# 4) Simple example dataset creation or loading
# -------------------------------------------------------------
def create_example_dataset():
    """
    Creates a small example dataset of social media posts
    with labels. In practice, replace this with real data.
    """
    # Suppose we have two classes: 'Positive' vs 'Negative'
↪    sentiment
    data = {
        "post": [
            "I love this new phone! It's amazing",
            "So disappointed with the service, never shopping here
↪            again",
            "Best experience ever, thank you!",
```

141

```python
            "I hate the slow delivery, very frustrating",
            "The product quality is great, totally recommend it",
            "Customer support was rude and unhelpful",
            "Awesome, everything works perfectly!",
            "Terrible experience, wasted my money"
        ],
        "label": [
            "Positive",
            "Negative",
            "Positive",
            "Negative",
            "Positive",
            "Negative",
            "Positive",
            "Negative"
        ],
    }
    df = pd.DataFrame(data)
    return df

# ---------------------------------------------------------------
# 5) Naive Bayes Training and Evaluation
# ---------------------------------------------------------------
def train_naive_bayes(X_train, y_train):
    """
    Trains a Gaussian Naive Bayes classifier on the given feature
    ↪    matrix
    and returns the fitted model.
    """
    nb_model = GaussianNB()
    nb_model.fit(X_train, y_train)
    return nb_model

def evaluate_naive_bayes(nb_model, X_test, y_test):
    """
    Evaluates the trained classifier on test data and prints
    classification report and confusion matrix.
    """
    y_pred = nb_model.predict(X_test)
    print("Classification Report:")
    print(classification_report(y_test, y_pred))
    print("Confusion Matrix:")
    print(confusion_matrix(y_test, y_pred))


# ---------------------------------------------------------------
# 6) Main script
# ---------------------------------------------------------------
def main():
    # Step A: Load or create data
    df = create_example_dataset()

    # Step B: Preprocess the posts
    df["post"] = df["post"].apply(preprocess_text)
```

142

```python
# Step C: Load GloVe embeddings
embeddings_dim = 50   # dimension can be 50, 100, 200, 300 for
↪  GloVe
glove_embeddings =
↪  load_glove_embeddings(embeddings_dim=embeddings_dim)

# Step D: Convert text into numerical feature vectors
X = create_embedding_features(df["post"].values,
↪  glove_embeddings, embeddings_dim=embeddings_dim)
y = df["label"].values

# Step E: Train-test split
X_train, X_test, y_train, y_test = train_test_split(X, y,

                                         ↪  test_size=0.3,

                                         ↪  random_state=42,
                                         stratify=y)

# Step F: Train Naive Bayes
nb_model = train_naive_bayes(X_train, y_train)

# Step G: Evaluate model
evaluate_naive_bayes(nb_model, X_test, y_test)

if __name__ == "__main__":
    main()
```

Key Implementation Details:

- **Loading GloVe Embeddings:** We rely on
  `load_glove_embeddings` to fetch and parse GloVe vectors,
  storing them in a dictionary keyed by words.

- **Text Preprocessing:** The function `preprocess_text` removes URLs, potential user mentions, punctuation, and stop-
  words to clean each post.

- **Embedding Conversion:** `create_embedding_features` takes
  tokenized text and averages the embeddings for all valid words.

- **Naive Bayes Classifier:** We use `GaussianNB` to model
  the real-valued embedding features. The training routine
  `train_naive_bayes` emphasizes the simplicity and speed of
  Naive Bayes.

143

- **Evaluation:** Finally, `evaluate_naive_bayes` uses a confusion matrix and classification report to interpret how textual meaning is captured in the classification process.

Chapter 30

Combining Naive Bayes with Ensemble Methods

While Naive Bayes is powerful by itself, it can also be integrated into ensemble classifiers such as Voting or Stacking. This chapter shows you how to combine NB with other models (like decision trees or logistic regression) in Python. You will build an ensemble pipeline, train multiple base learners, and then combine their predictions. By walking through code examples, you will see how NB's probabilistic approach complements other algorithms, boosting overall accuracy for complex datasets.

- First, we load and split a dataset into training and testing sets.

- Next, we train a standalone Naive Bayes classifier to highlight its probabilistic approach.

- We then construct a Voting ensemble with multiple classifiers (including Naive Bayes).

- Finally, we demonstrate a Stacking classifier to see how meta-models can learn from base learners' outputs.

Python Code Snippet

```python
import numpy as np
from sklearn.model_selection import train_test_split
from sklearn.datasets import load_iris
from sklearn.naive_bayes import GaussianNB
from sklearn.tree import DecisionTreeClassifier
from sklearn.linear_model import LogisticRegression
from sklearn.ensemble import VotingClassifier, StackingClassifier
from sklearn.metrics import accuracy_score, classification_report

def run_naive_bayes(X_train, X_test, y_train, y_test):
    """
    Train and evaluate a standalone Naive Bayes classifier.
    """
    print("---- Naive Bayes Classifier ----")
    nb_model = GaussianNB()
    nb_model.fit(X_train, y_train)

    y_pred = nb_model.predict(X_test)
    acc = accuracy_score(y_test, y_pred)
    print("Naive Bayes Accuracy:", acc)
    print("Classification Report:")
    print(classification_report(y_test, y_pred))
    return acc

def run_voting_ensemble(X_train, X_test, y_train, y_test):
    """
    Construct and evaluate a Voting ensemble that includes Naive
    ↪ Bayes,
    Decision Tree, and Logistic Regression as base learners.
    """
    print("---- Voting Ensemble ----")
    nb = GaussianNB()
    dt = DecisionTreeClassifier(random_state=42)
    lr = LogisticRegression(max_iter=200, solver='liblinear',
    ↪ random_state=42)

    voting_ensemble = VotingClassifier(
        estimators=[('nb', nb), ('dt', dt), ('lr', lr)],
        voting='soft'  # 'soft' uses predicted probabilities for
        ↪ voting
    )
    voting_ensemble.fit(X_train, y_train)

    y_pred = voting_ensemble.predict(X_test)
    acc = accuracy_score(y_test, y_pred)
    print("Voting Ensemble Accuracy:", acc)
    print("Classification Report:")
    print(classification_report(y_test, y_pred))
    return acc
```

```python
def run_stacking_ensemble(X_train, X_test, y_train, y_test):
    """
    Construct and evaluate a Stacking ensemble with Naive Bayes,
    Decision Tree, and Logistic Regression. The meta-learner is a
    ↪  Logistic Regression.
    """
    print("---- Stacking Ensemble ----")
    nb = GaussianNB()
    dt = DecisionTreeClassifier(random_state=42)
    lr = LogisticRegression(max_iter=200, solver='liblinear',
    ↪  random_state=42)

    # The base estimators
    estimators = [
        ('nb', nb),
        ('dt', dt),
        ('lr', lr)
    ]

    # The final estimator (meta-model)
    meta_estimator = LogisticRegression(max_iter=200,
    ↪  solver='liblinear', random_state=42)

    stacking_ensemble = StackingClassifier(
        estimators=estimators,
        final_estimator=meta_estimator
    )
    stacking_ensemble.fit(X_train, y_train)

    y_pred = stacking_ensemble.predict(X_test)
    acc = accuracy_score(y_test, y_pred)
    print("Stacking Ensemble Accuracy:", acc)
    print("Classification Report:")
    print(classification_report(y_test, y_pred))
    return acc

def main():
    # 1. Load the Iris dataset (4 features, 3 classes) for
    ↪  simplicity
    data = load_iris()
    X = data.data
    y = data.target

    # 2. Split the dataset into train/test sets
    X_train, X_test, y_train, y_test = train_test_split(X, y,

                                               ↪  test_size=0.3,

                                               ↪  random_state=42,
                                               stratify=y)

    # 3. Run and compare different approaches
```

147

```
# (A) Standalone Naive Bayes
nb_acc = run_naive_bayes(X_train, X_test, y_train, y_test)

# (B) Voting ensemble with NB, Decision Tree, and Logistic
↪  Regression
vote_acc = run_voting_ensemble(X_train, X_test, y_train, y_test)

# (C) Stacking ensemble with NB, Decision Tree, and Logistic
↪  Regression
stack_acc = run_stacking_ensemble(X_train, X_test, y_train,
↪  y_test)

# 4. Print a simple comparison summary
print("---- Accuracy Comparison ----")
print(f"Naive Bayes Only: {nb_acc:.3f}")
print(f"Voting Ensemble: {vote_acc:.3f}")
print(f"Stacking Ensemble: {stack_acc:.3f}")

if __name__ == "__main__":
    main()
```

Key Implementation Details:

- **Naive Bayes Emphasis:** The function `run_naive_bayes` shows the typical workflow for training and evaluating a standalone Naive Bayes model. It fits `GaussianNB` to the data and prints performance metrics.

- **Voting Classifier:** In `run_voting_ensemble`, we combine Naive Bayes, a decision tree, and logistic regression in a `VotingClassifier` with soft voting. This blends individual model predictions into a single consensus.

- **Stacking Classifier:** The `run_stacking_ensemble` function illustrates meta-learning: base learners (including Naive Bayes) feed their outputs to a `LogisticRegression` meta-model that refines final predictions.

- **Performance Comparison:** We output separate accuracies and classification reports for each approach, showcasing how the ensemble methods often (though not always) outperform a standalone Naive Bayes.

- **Example Dataset:** We use Iris for demonstration due to its simplicity. Larger real-world datasets would likely benefit even more from ensemble techniques that include Naive Bayes as one of the base learners.

Chapter 31

Scaling Naive Bayes to Big Data with Apache Spark

For very large datasets, you may need distributed computing. This chapter details using PySpark's Naive Bayes implementation on a cluster. You will learn data ingestion into Spark DataFrames, feature extraction (HashingTF, IDF), and the Spark ML pipeline for training a Naive Bayes model. The Python code exemplifies building a script that runs on a multi-node cluster, discussing the trade-offs of distributed training and tips for optimizing memory usage in a Spark environment.

Python Code Snippet

```
#!/usr/bin/env python

"""
Scaling Naive Bayes to Big Data with Apache Spark
--------------------------------------------------
This script demonstrates how to build a Naive Bayes text
↪ classification pipeline
using PySpark on a large dataset. It includes data ingestion, text
↪ feature
extraction with TF-IDF, model training, and evaluation. Emphasis is
↪ placed on
the Naive Bayes portion.
```

```python
import sys
from pyspark.sql import SparkSession
from pyspark.sql.functions import col
from pyspark.ml import Pipeline
from pyspark.ml.feature import StringIndexer, Tokenizer,
↪   StopWordsRemover, HashingTF, IDF
from pyspark.ml.classification import NaiveBayes
from pyspark.ml.evaluation import MulticlassClassificationEvaluator

def main():
    """
    Main function to create a Spark session, read data, build a
    ↪   Naive Bayes pipeline,
    train the model, and evaluate performance on the test set.
    """

    # -------------------------------------------------------------
    # 1) Initialize Spark Session
    # -------------------------------------------------------------
    spark = SparkSession.builder \
        .appName("NaiveBayesBigDataExample") \
        .getOrCreate()

    # Increase log level to WARN to reduce console output if
    ↪   desired.
    spark.sparkContext.setLogLevel("WARN")

    # -------------------------------------------------------------
    # 2) Read in Sample Data
    # -------------------------------------------------------------
    # For demonstration, let's assume 'text' column holds raw text,
    # and 'label_str' column holds the label. Replace paths as
    ↪   needed.
    # In a real scenario, the dataset could be very large
    ↪   (gigabytes/terabytes).
    data_path = "YOUR_DATA.csv"  # Edit with actual data path

    # Example schema (depends on your dataset):
    # CSV might have columns: label_str,text
    # e.g., "spam","Free entry in 2 a wkly comp to win..."
    df = spark.read.csv(data_path, header=True, inferSchema=True)

    # Drop any rows missing text or label
    df = df.na.drop(subset=["text", "label_str"])

    # -------------------------------------------------------------
```

150

```python
# 3) String Indexing for Label
# ----------------------------------------------------------
label_indexer = StringIndexer(inputCol="label_str",
↪   outputCol="label")


# ----------------------------------------------------------
# 4) Tokenizer and StopWordsRemover
# ----------------------------------------------------------
# Splits raw text into words
tokenizer = Tokenizer(inputCol="text", outputCol="tokens")

# Removes common words
stop_remover = StopWordsRemover(inputCol="tokens",
↪   outputCol="filtered_tokens")


# ----------------------------------------------------------
# 5) HashingTF for Feature Transformation
# ----------------------------------------------------------
# HashingTF transforms tokenized text into term frequency
↪   vectors
hashing_tf = HashingTF(
    inputCol="filtered_tokens",
    outputCol="rawFeatures",
    numFeatures=4096   # Adjust feature dimension based on
    ↪   dataset
)


# ----------------------------------------------------------
# 6) IDF to Down-Weight Common Tokens
# ----------------------------------------------------------
# IDF transforms term frequency vectors (raw features) into
↪   TF-IDF vectors
idf = IDF(
    inputCol="rawFeatures",
    outputCol="features"
)


# ----------------------------------------------------------
# 7) Naive Bayes Classifier
# ----------------------------------------------------------
# We configure the NaiveBayes model to handle multi-class
↪   classification
# using multinomial distribution (default).
nb_classifier = NaiveBayes(
    featuresCol="features",
    labelCol="label",
    predictionCol="prediction",
    modelType="multinomial",  # or "bernoulli" if features are
    ↪   binary
    smoothing=1.0
)

# ----------------------------------------------------------
```

```python
# 8) Set Up Pipeline
# ------------------------------------------------------------
# The pipeline will execute each stage in the specified order.
pipeline = Pipeline(stages=[
    label_indexer,
    tokenizer,
    stop_remover,
    hashing_tf,
    idf,
    nb_classifier
])


# ------------------------------------------------------------
# 9) Train-Test Split
# ------------------------------------------------------------
# For large data, it's essential to ensure the split returns
# ↪   manageable subsets.
train_df, test_df = df.randomSplit([0.8, 0.2], seed=42)


# ------------------------------------------------------------
# 10) Training the Pipeline
# ------------------------------------------------------------
# The fit() method automatically runs all stages, culminating in
# ↪   a trained model.
model = pipeline.fit(train_df)


# ------------------------------------------------------------
# 11) Evaluate the Model
# ------------------------------------------------------------
# Use the trained pipeline model to make predictions on the test
# ↪   set.
predictions = model.transform(test_df)

# Evaluate the predictions with a
# ↪   MulticlassClassificationEvaluator
evaluator_accuracy = MulticlassClassificationEvaluator(
    labelCol="label",
    predictionCol="prediction",
    metricName="accuracy"
)
accuracy = evaluator_accuracy.evaluate(predictions)

evaluator_f1 = MulticlassClassificationEvaluator(
    labelCol="label",
    predictionCol="prediction",
    metricName="f1"
)
f1_score = evaluator_f1.evaluate(predictions)

print(f"Test Accuracy  = {accuracy:.4f}")
print(f"Test F1-Score = {f1_score:.4f}")

# ------------------------------------------------------------
```

```
# 12) Additional Considerations
# ------------------------------------------------------------
# For memory optimization on large clusters:
#   - Increase executor memory and cores.
#   - Use efficient file formats like Parquet.
#   - Utilize Spark's built-in caching or checkpointing for
↪   intermediate DataFrames.

    spark.stop()

if __name__ == "__main__":
    main()
```

Key Implementation Details:

- **Data Ingestion and Spark Context:** The `SparkSession` is created to manage a cluster's resources. Ensure you configure memory and executor settings as needed for large-scale data.

- **Pipeline Construction:** We use `StringIndexer` to convert string labels to numeric form, then `Tokenizer` and `StopWordsRemover` to preprocess text. Subsequently, `HashingTF` and `IDF` build TF-IDF features. Finally, the `NaiveBayes` classifier trains on these features.

- **Naive Bayes Emphasis:** The script uses the PySpark `NaiveBayes` model. You can tweak `smoothing` and `modelType` (multinomial vs. bernoulli) based on dataset characteristics.

- **Multi-node Training:** By submitting with `spark-submit` on a cluster manager (e.g., YARN or Standalone), the pipeline can distribute tasks. `SparkSession` orchestrates dataset partitioning, transformations, and training across worker nodes.

- **Evaluation Metrics:** We employ `MulticlassClassificationEvaluator` for accuracy and F1 score. Additional metrics (precision, recall) can be computed similarly.

- **Memory and Efficiency Tips:**
  - Use columnar formats like Parquet for faster I/O.
  - Leverage `cache()` or `persist()` for repeated DataFrame use.

153

– Partition large datasets optimally to balance parallelism and overhead.

Chapter 32

Automatic Question Classification with Naive Bayes

In this chapter, you will classify questions by type (e.g., who, what, when, where, why, how). After collecting labeled question data, you will extract lexical features (keywords) or syntactic structures (part-of-speech tags). A MultinomialNB or BernoulliNB classifier can then learn to predict which category a question belongs to, which is useful for automated FAQ routing or conversational systems. Will guide you through text preparation, feature design, model training, and help illuminate common pitfalls when dealing with short question texts.

- Gather a labeled set of questions, each annotated with its category (e.g., "what," "who," "where," "why," etc.).

- Preprocess the text by lowercasing, removing punctuation, and optionally applying additional NLP techniques such as tokenization or part-of-speech tagging.

- Convert the cleaned text into numerical features using methods like bag-of-words or TF-IDF vectors.

- Train a `MultinomialNB` or `BernoulliNB` model to classify new questions according to their type.

- Evaluate results with metrics such as accuracy, precision, recall, F1-score, and confusion matrices for deeper insight.

Python Code Snippet

```python
import re
import random
import numpy as np
from sklearn.feature_extraction.text import CountVectorizer
from sklearn.model_selection import train_test_split
from sklearn.naive_bayes import MultinomialNB, BernoulliNB
from sklearn.metrics import classification_report, confusion_matrix

def preprocess_text(text):
    # Convert text to lowercase
    text = text.lower()
    # Remove punctuation using a regular expression
    text = re.sub(r'[^\w\s]', '', text)
    return text

def main():
    # Example labeled dataset: (question_text, question_type)
    question_data = [
        ("Who discovered penicillin?", "who"),
        ("When was the Eiffel Tower built?", "when"),
        ("Why is the sky blue?", "why"),
        ("How do I cook pasta correctly?", "how"),
        ("What is the capital of France?", "what"),
        ("Where can I find good coffee?", "where"),
        ("Who is the current President of the US?", "who"),
        ("When does the next train arrive?", "when"),
        ("Why do leaves change color in the fall?", "why"),
        ("How can I reset my password?", "how"),
        ("What is machine learning?", "what"),
        ("Where is the Taj Mahal located?", "where"),
        ("Which planet is known as the Red Planet?", "which"),
        ("Which programming language should I learn first?",
         "which")
    ]

    # Separate text and labels
    texts = [entry[0] for entry in question_data]
    labels = [entry[1] for entry in question_data]

    # Preprocess each question
    texts = [preprocess_text(t) for t in texts]

    # Split into train and test sets
    X_train, X_test, y_train, y_test = train_test_split(
        texts, labels, test_size=0.3, random_state=42,
        stratify=labels
    )

    # Convert text data to feature vectors
    vectorizer = CountVectorizer()
```

```
X_train_vec = vectorizer.fit_transform(X_train)
X_test_vec = vectorizer.transform(X_test)

# --------------------------------------------
# Train with Multinomial Naive Bayes
# --------------------------------------------
mnb = MultinomialNB()
mnb.fit(X_train_vec, y_train)
y_pred_mnb = mnb.predict(X_test_vec)

print("MultinomialNB Classification Report:")
print(classification_report(y_test, y_pred_mnb))
print("Confusion Matrix:")
print(confusion_matrix(y_test, y_pred_mnb))

# --------------------------------------------
# Train with Bernoulli Naive Bayes
# --------------------------------------------
bnb = BernoulliNB()
bnb.fit(X_train_vec, y_train)
y_pred_bnb = bnb.predict(X_test_vec)

print("\nBernoulliNB Classification Report:")
print(classification_report(y_test, y_pred_bnb))
print("Confusion Matrix:")
print(confusion_matrix(y_test, y_pred_bnb))

if __name__ == "__main__":
    main()
```

Key Implementation Details:

- **Data Preparation:** We defined a small labeled dataset of questions and their expected categories. Each question is processed by the `preprocess_text` function, which lowercases and strips punctuation.

- **Feature Extraction:** The `CountVectorizer` transforms each question into a bag-of-words representation. This numeric encoding is essential for training the Naive Bayes models.

- **Naive Bayes Classifiers:** We employ both `MultinomialNB` and `BernoulliNB` to show how different NB variants handle feature distributions. Each model is trained by calling `fit` on the transformed training data.

- **Evaluation:** We generate predictions using `predict` on the test data and compare them to the ground truth using metrics like precision, recall, and F1-score from `classification_report`, as well as a `confusion_matrix` for detailed insight.

- **Stratified Splitting:** By using `train_test_split` with `stratify=labels`, we ensure the class proportions remain consistent between training and test sets, which is crucial for balanced evaluation.

Chapter 33

Real-time Anomaly Detection in IoT Sensor Data with Naive Bayes

Finally, you will implement an anomaly detection module for IoT sensor streams using Naive Bayes. Generating or collecting normal sensor signals, you will fit a GaussianNB model on features such as temperature, pressure, or motion readings. The model learns typical ranges and correlations of sensor values. When new measurements deviate significantly, the classifier flags them as anomalies. You will see how to continuously update or partially retrain the model in Python to handle sensor drift and maintain reliable detection over time.

Python Code Snippet

```python
import numpy as np
from sklearn.naive_bayes import GaussianNB
from sklearn.metrics import accuracy_score
import matplotlib.pyplot as plt

def generate_synthetic_iot_stream(n_batches=10, batch_size=100,
                                  anomaly_ratio=0.1, seed=42):
    """
```

Simulates an IoT sensor data stream in small batches. Each batch
contains mostly 'normal' data and a fraction of 'anomalies'.

Normal data is drawn from a multivariate Gaussian distribution
with some fixed mean and covariance. Anomalies are drawn from
an offset distribution that does not overlap significantly with
the normal ranges.

:param n_batches: Number of batches to yield.
:param batch_size: Number of samples per batch.
:param anomaly_ratio: Proportion of anomalies in each batch.
:param seed: Random state seed for reproducibility.
:return: Yields a tuple (X_batch, y_batch) for each batch.
"""

```python
np.random.seed(seed)

# Mean and covariance for 'normal' data (temp, pressure, motion)
normal_mean = np.array([25.0, 1013.0, 5.0])
normal_cov = np.diag([1.0, 2.0, 0.5])  # Somewhat arbitrary

# Mean for anomalies (offset artificially)
anomaly_mean = np.array([35.0, 1025.0, 15.0])
anomaly_cov = np.diag([1.0, 2.0, 0.5])

for i in range(n_batches):
    # Generate normal data
    n_normal = int(batch_size * (1 - anomaly_ratio))
    X_normal = np.random.multivariate_normal(normal_mean,
    ↪  normal_cov, n_normal)
    y_normal = np.zeros(n_normal, dtype=int)  # label '0' for
    ↪  normal

    # Generate anomalies
    n_anomalies = batch_size - n_normal
    X_anomaly = np.random.multivariate_normal(anomaly_mean,
    ↪  anomaly_cov, n_anomalies)
    y_anomaly = np.ones(n_anomalies, dtype=int)  # label '1' for
    ↪  anomaly

    # Combine and shuffle
    X_batch = np.vstack((X_normal, X_anomaly))
    y_batch = np.hstack((y_normal, y_anomaly))

    # Shuffle batch
    indices = np.arange(batch_size)
    np.random.shuffle(indices)
    X_batch = X_batch[indices]
    y_batch = y_batch[indices]

    yield X_batch, y_batch

def main():
    """
```

```python
    Main routine that demonstrates real-time anomaly detection
    with a Naive Bayes classifier (GaussianNB) by simulating
    partial (streaming) updates to handle sensor drift.
    """
    # Initialize the GaussianNB model
    # We'll specify the classes [0, 1] so partial_fit
    # knows about both normal and anomaly classes upfront.
    model = GaussianNB()
    classes = np.array([0, 1])

    # We simulate that we only have normal data initially for
    ↪   training.
    # Then new data (including anomalies) arrives in small batches.

    # First, simulate an 'initial' batch of normal data for initial
    ↪   fit.
    # We'll call this the 'historical' normal data to start with.
    np.random.seed(123)
    initial_normal_samples = 300
    normal_mean = np.array([25.0, 1013.0, 5.0])
    normal_cov = np.diag([1.0, 2.0, 0.5])
    X_init = np.random.multivariate_normal(normal_mean, normal_cov,
    ↪   initial_normal_samples)
    y_init = np.zeros(initial_normal_samples, dtype=int)   # 0 =>
    ↪   normal

    # Perform the first partial_fit call with classes
    model.partial_fit(X_init, y_init, classes=classes)

    # Prepare to track performance
    all_predictions = []
    all_labels = []

    # We define a threshold on the predicted probability of
    ↪   belonging
    # to class '0' (normal). If p(normal) < threshold => anomaly.
    anomaly_threshold = 0.5

    # Simulate streaming IoT data in multiple batches:
    for batch_idx, (X_batch, y_batch) in
    ↪   enumerate(generate_synthetic_iot_stream(
            n_batches=8, batch_size=50, anomaly_ratio=0.2,
            ↪   seed=999)):
        # Predict probabilities for each class
        # prob_of_normal is column 0 (since class=0).
        prob_of_normal = model.predict_proba(X_batch)[:, 0]

        # Label as anomaly if p(normal) < threshold
        predicted_labels = (prob_of_normal <
        ↪   anomaly_threshold).astype(int)

        all_predictions.extend(predicted_labels)
        all_labels.extend(y_batch)
```

```
# Now, we adapt the model. Suppose we assume we do get
# some labels eventually (delayed or partially). For
# demonstration, we do partial_fit with the entire batch
# so the model can 'learn' from new normal data and
↳  anomalies.
model.partial_fit(X_batch, y_batch, classes=classes)

batch_accuracy = accuracy_score(y_batch, predicted_labels)
print(f"Batch {batch_idx+1} - Accuracy:
↳  {batch_accuracy:.3f}")

overall_accuracy = accuracy_score(all_labels, all_predictions)
print(f"Overall streaming accuracy: {overall_accuracy:.3f}")

# Finally, display a simple scatter plot of the last batch
# to visualize normal vs. anomaly predictions (for 2 features).
# For demonstration, we only pick the first two sensors:
# (temperature, pressure).
if len(X_batch) > 0:
    plt.figure(figsize=(6,6))
    # Plot normal predictions in green, anomaly predictions in
    ↳  red
    anomaly_mask = (predicted_labels == 1)
    normal_mask = (predicted_labels == 0)

    plt.scatter(X_batch[normal_mask, 0], X_batch[normal_mask,
    ↳  1],
                label="Predicted Normal", c='g', alpha=0.7)
    plt.scatter(X_batch[anomaly_mask, 0], X_batch[anomaly_mask,
    ↳  1],
                label="Predicted Anomaly", c='r', alpha=0.7)

    plt.title("Predictions in Last Batch (Temp vs Pressure)")
    plt.xlabel("Temperature")
    plt.ylabel("Pressure")
    plt.legend()
    plt.show()

if __name__ == "__main__":
    main()
```

Key Implementation Details:

- **Data Simulation**: A function `generate_synthetic_iot_stream` produces small batches of normal and anomalous samples to mimic sensor readings arriving in real time.

- **Naive Bayes Model**: We use `GaussianNB` for its handling of continuous features (temperature, pressure, etc.). The initial call to `partial_fit` needs the `classes` argument to register both normal and anomaly labels.

- **Anomaly Threshold**: After computing the posterior probabilities, we flag any sample as anomalous if the predicted probability of class 0 (normal) is below a chosen threshold (e.g., 0.5).

- **Online Updates**: The Naive Bayes model is updated after each batch via `partial_fit` to incorporate newly arriving samples, handling sensor drift.

- **Evaluation**: We accumulate predictions on each streaming batch, measure accuracy, and in the end visualize the final batch to see how anomalies are distributed relative to normal data in a 2D projection.

www.ingramcontent.com/pod-product-compliance
Lightning Source LLC
LaVergne TN
LVHW051340050326
832903LV00031B/3651